Color Woodblock **PRINTMAKING**

Color Woodblock
PRINTMAKING
The Traditional Method of Ukiyo-e

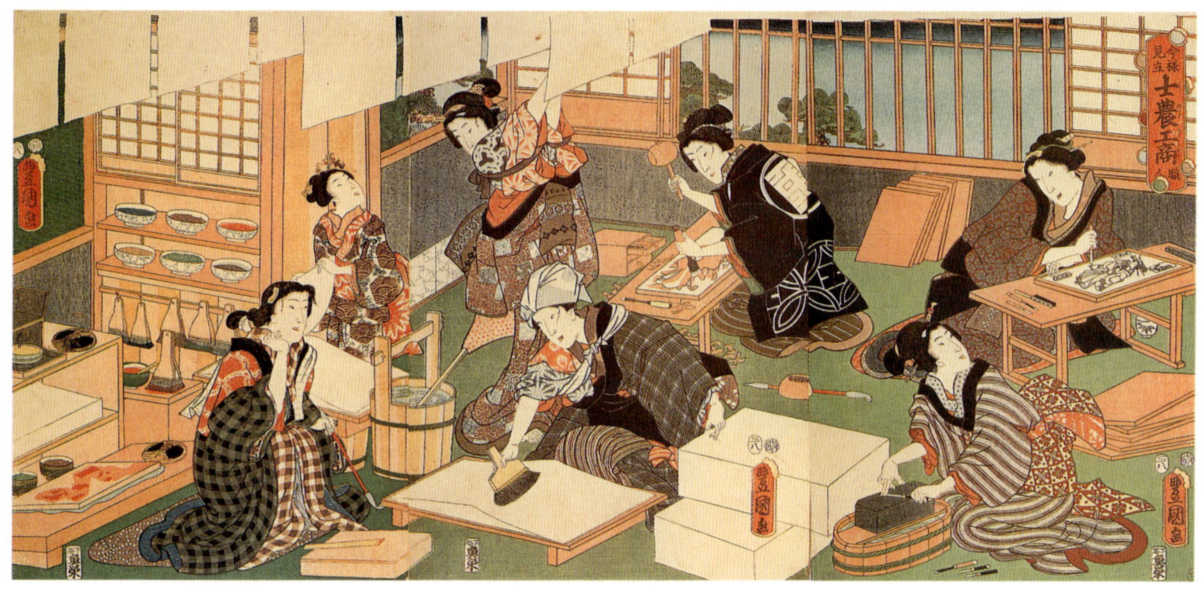

Margaret Miller Kanada

SHUFUNOTOMO CO., LTD.

First printing, 1989

Design: Nishimura Momoyo

Published by
Shufunotomo Co., Ltd.
2-9, Kanda Surugadai, Chiyoda-ku, Tokyo, 101 Japan

ISBN: 4-07-974653-9
Printed in Japan

ACKNOWLEGEMENTS

First, I would like to thank Prof. Suzuki Jūzō for his scholarly advice and generous loan of several prints photographed to illustrate this book.

Tokyo Broadcasting Systems Inc. (TBS) permitted the photographing of original *Hokusai* woodblocks (during their exhibition in Tokyo on loan from The Boston Museum of Fine Arts). Thanks also to The Art Institute of Chicago, The Boston Museum of Fine Arts, The British Museum, Ishukankokai, National Diet Library, Tokyo Metropolitan Central Library, and The Tokyo National Museum for permission to use photos of woodblock prints and books in their collections.

My deep appreciation also extends to Nagai Kazuhiko and my husband, Shin, who patiently encouraged this project through to completion.

All Japanese names in this book are given in Japanese style: first, family name (or sometimes artistic school/shop name), followed by the individual's given name. In the case of artist's names, ALL-CAPITAL LETTERS indicate the given (or professional) name by which the pre-modern artist is commonly known.

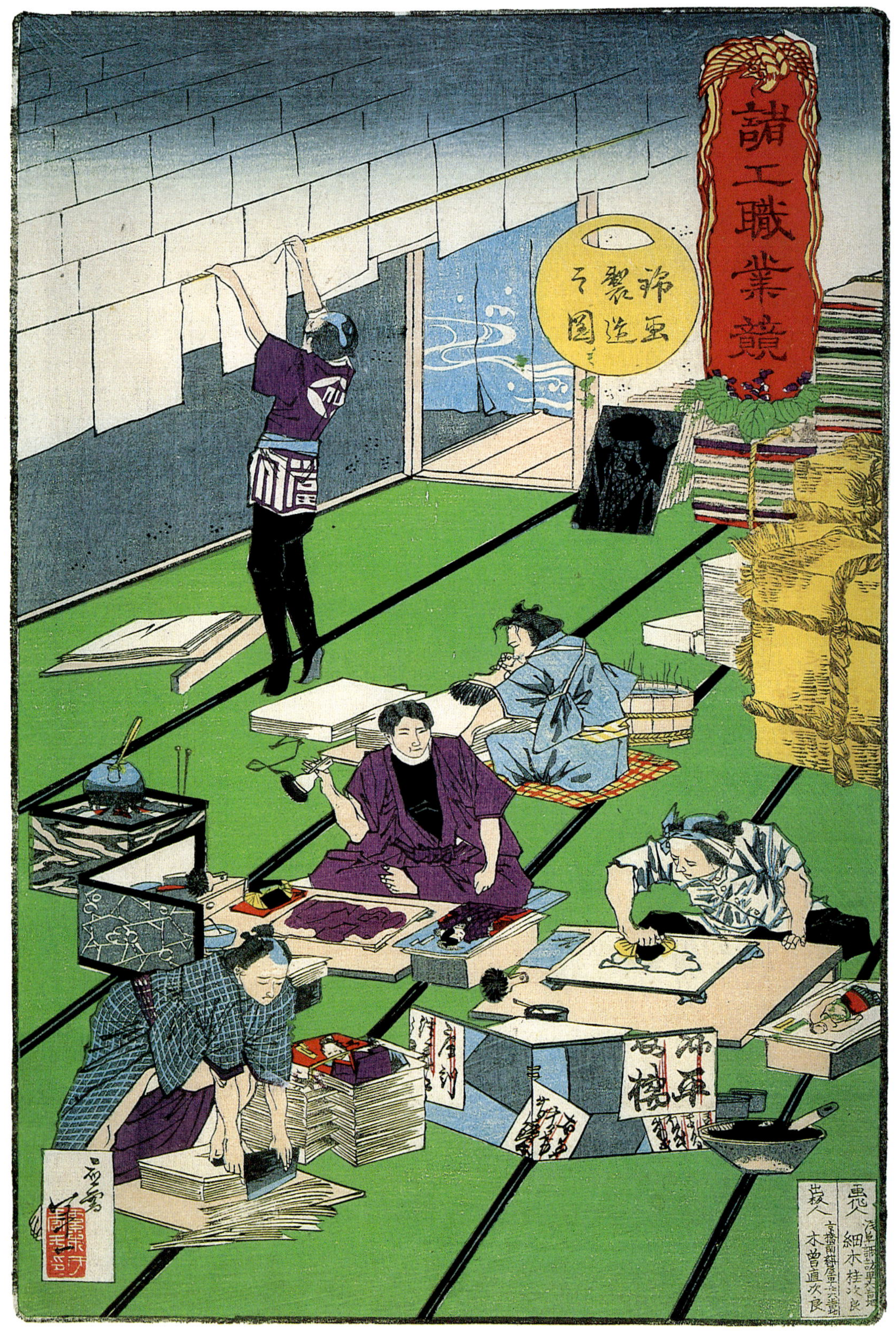

6

CONTENTS

Preface   8

Historical Introduction   10

What is *Ukiyo-e?*   10
Historical Background of Japanese
   Woodblock Printing   12
The Beginnings of Color Printing   13
Full-Color Woodblock Printing
   and *Nishiki-e*   14

Making a Full-Color Woodblock Print   21

The Paper Used for Woodblock Prints   21
The Artist's Master Design   25
The Publisher   25
The Woodblock Carver   29
Carving the Keyblock from
   the Artist's Design   30
Correcting the Woodblock   33
Carving the Rest of the Woodblock Set   34
The Printer   35
Full-Color Trial Proofs and Final
   Correction of Woodblocks   35
The Pigments   37
Preparing the Paper   38
Readying the Block and Applying Pigment   41
Printing   42
The Printing Order of Woodblocks
   for an Edition   46
Trimming the Finished Print   72
Selling the Prints   74
The Fate of the Woodblocks   77

Full-Color Woodblock Printmaking Today   79

Bibliography   83
Index   85

"Producing Full-color Woodblock Prints" in the series "Mirror of Various Artisan Trades" (*Shokōshokugyō kagami*), 1880.
Hosoki TOSHIICHI. Full-color, *ōban* print. Private collection.
     Steps in making a full-color woodblock print are compressed into one depiction. In the background are stacks of woodblocks and bundles of new paper. One artisan applies sizing while one hangs up the sheets to dry. Two printers at center (behind low screens) apply pigment to a block and take an impression by rubbing with a *baren*. At front an assistant trims the margins of finished prints.

In the late nineteenth century Europeans and Americans discovered the Japanese *ukiyo-e* woodblock print. This was just as its heyday, the 18th through mid-19th century, was passing. The enthusiasm of western collectors in that period was not matched until the 1960's when interest in *ukiyo-e* prints revived to reach its present level. At the same time many Japanese began to re-evaluate what had been dismissed in Japan as inexpensive, ephemeral manifestations of plebeian culture.

Of course, today, prints command museum prices. Major collections of oriental art throughout the world treasure them as works of art and the serious objects of study. While the finest *ukiyo-e* prints have passed out of the collector's market and into permanent public holdings, the interest in minor artists and later, 19th century prints continues to grow. Modern reproductions of old prints using the traditional woodblock print techniques have enjoyed popularity. One of the remarkable aspects of modern Japan is the survival of traditional craft techniques, even though the historic circumstances and creative impulse that engendered them have disappeared.

This book, an introduction to full-color woodblock printmaking, draws on the experiences of the living craftsmen who still know how to make traditional prints. The historical discussion relies on the extensive research of Japanese and western scholars of *ukiyo-e*. Like other skills handed down from master to apprentice with only fragmentary written records, it is hard to know if certain details of the woodblock printmaking process we observe

today may be modern innovations. By using extant woodblock prints and book illustrations that actually depict the making and selling of prints in the 18th and 19th centuries, along with photos of modern craftsmen making a reproduction of a full-color print, I hope to give a clearer understanding of the process in the old days.

Detail from "A Parody of [the Four Social Classes] Samurai, Farmers, Artisans, and Merchants in the Latest Fashions: Artisans [i.e. Printmakers]" (*Imayō mitate shinōkōsho shokunin*), 1857. Utagawa KUNISADA (signed himself TOYOKUNI [III.]). Full-color, *ōban* prints. Published by Uoya Eikichi. Private collection.
The blockcarver (at r.) clears areas with chisel and mallet, while printers apply sizing and hang up the sheets to dry.
Despite the incongruity of replacing the male artisans with beauties, Kunisada seems to have depicted printmaking with care for realistic details. However, borrowing from an earlier print composition by Utamaro (also reproduced, see pp. 28, 39) has placed them all at work in one studio (here apparently the second-floor above the publisher's shop). Documentation is scarce about early working conditions, but sources suggest the blockcarver's and the printer's workshops were different.   (See title page for entire scene.)

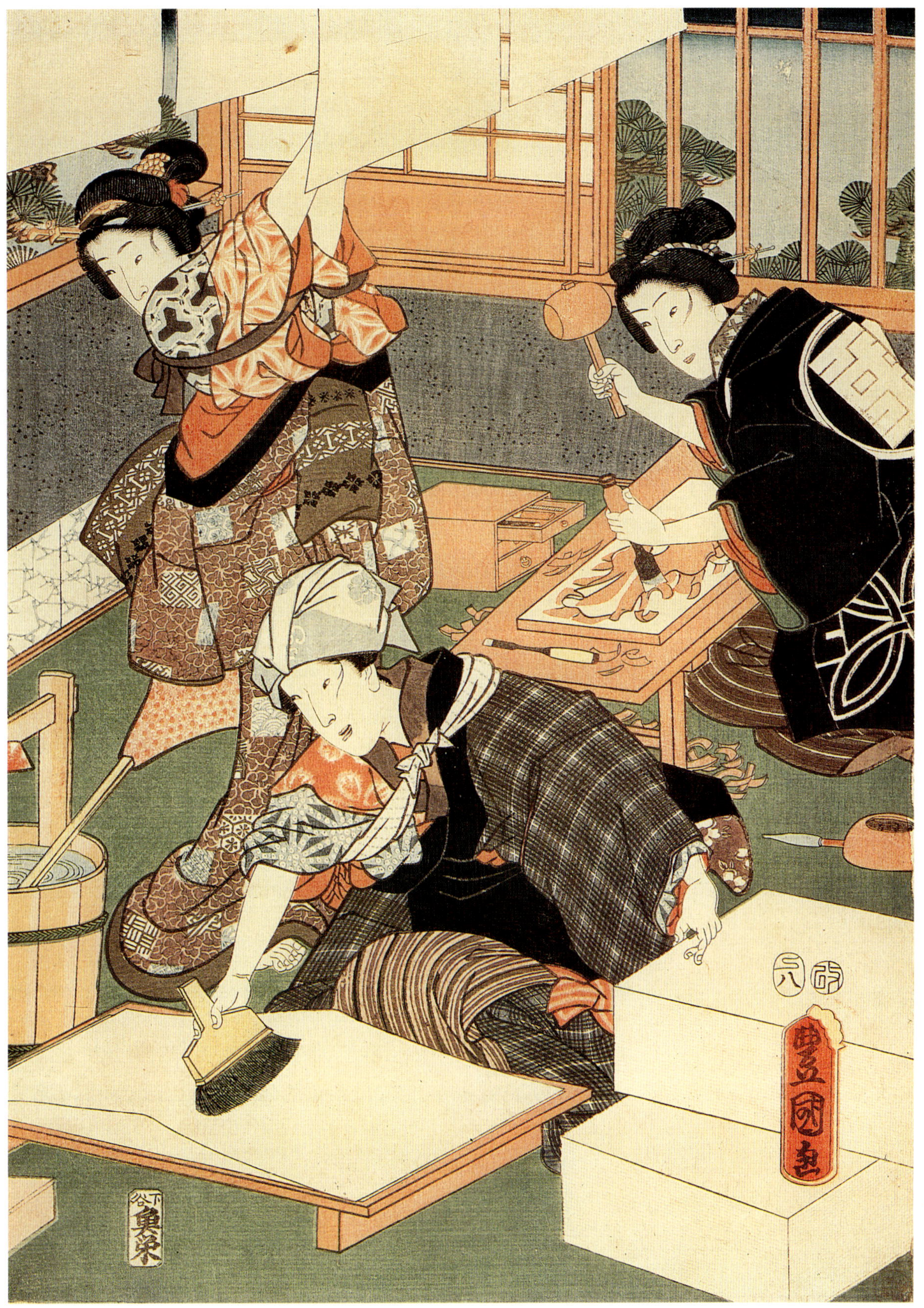

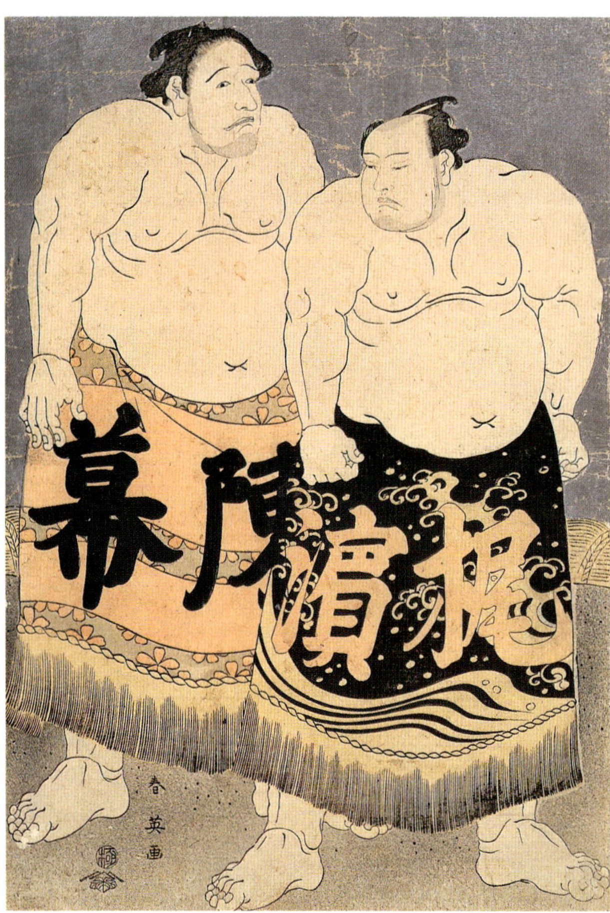

"*Sumo* Wrestlers: Kajihama and Jinmaku," late 1790's.
Katsukawa SHUN'EI.
Full-color, *ōban* print. The Tokyo National Museum.

Historical Introduction

What is *Ukiyo-e?*

Today we find *ukiyo-e* sometimes used as a synonym for woodblock prints, although the term properly refers to a style in which artists produced many paintings as well. Some *ukiyo-e* artists produced only paintings and no print designs. Nevertheless, from the time of the earliest identifiable *ukiyo-e* artist, Hishikawa Moronobu (active in the 1680's and 1690's), *ukiyo-e* has included prints or printed book illustrations. *Ukiyo-e* artists responded to a growing demand for their work that could not be met by paintings alone. Printmaking, it need hardly be repeated, by replicating an image many times—using inexpensive paper and pigments—reduced the cost far below an equivalent visual treatment of the subject in a painting or drawing. A print was well within the reach of prosperous townspeople: merchants, artisans and the lower-ranks of the samurai bureaucrats and retainers.

It is sometimes said that *ukiyo-e* prints were the same as modern calendar-girl pinups or posters of the latest popstar. This obscures the fact that *ukiyo-e*, certainly before the mid-19th century, never reached the masses of Japanese who were the peasant farmers and fishermen in the villages. Yet *ukiyo-e* and especially *ukiyo-e* woodblock prints can indeed be called an early popular art form in terms of audience and subject matter. Unlike other Japanese painters of the time, especially in the Tosa and Kanō schools, *ukiyo-e* artists made no claim to patrons from among the old aristocracy or the governing shogun and warrior elite. Most print buyers were, in effect, middle-class. They lived in or had come to visit "the big city", pre-eminently the capital at Edo (present-day Tokyo), which gave its name to the Edo period (1603–1868). These were people who enjoyed the pleasures of a money economy and an urban, popular culture that in many ways resembles life in modern Japan. Commerce flourished, along with theater, prostitution, and other services such as restaurants. *Sumo* wrestling matches attracted crowds. Publishing, because many were literate, was a profitable business and competition appears to have been cutthroat. Without the proliferation of today's electronic media, commerical prints by *ukiyo-e* artists (along with the woodblock illustrations for books and privately commissioned prints designed by many of the same *ukiyo-e* artists) were an indispensable aspect of townspeople's visual and cultural experience.

Put simply, the term *"ukiyo-e"* means "depictions" (or *"e"*) of popular pleasures of town life. *"Ukiyo"* carries the nuance colored by a Buddhist world-view that such pleasures bring pain because we are unable to disentangle ourselves emotionally from this our transitory, or literally, "floating world," of human existence. *Ukiyo-e* can most easily be recognized from other art of the period by its subject matter.

The subject categories of Edo *ukiyo-e* prints with a few exceptions were limited: erotica, Kabuki actors (depicted as characters *en rôle*), *sumo* wrestlers, and beautiful women (courtesans and entertainers of the pleasure quarters as well as the neighborhood beauties such as the tea-shop waitress Ohisa). Later, mainly from the nineteenth century, *ukiyo-e* artists produced views of Edo or landscapes of scenic spots favored by travelers and pilgrims, and occasionally themes of "birds and flowers" and historic legend. While standard subjects, particularly actors and beauties, did not change significantly for years, individual print designs were always susceptible to what was popular at the moment. A major preoccupation was to depict the latest kimono fabrics and hairstyles. Artists constantly borrowed (or stole) successful compositions and stylistic ideas from each other. *Ukiyo-e* print compositions and, to an extent, techniques and formats, were given to fads and almost as transitory as the current Kabuki play run or the latest gossip.

The Edo shogunal government, in its initially effective attempts to preserve social order, strove to prevent not only political dissent but ostentatious display. Obvious wealth in the hands of the

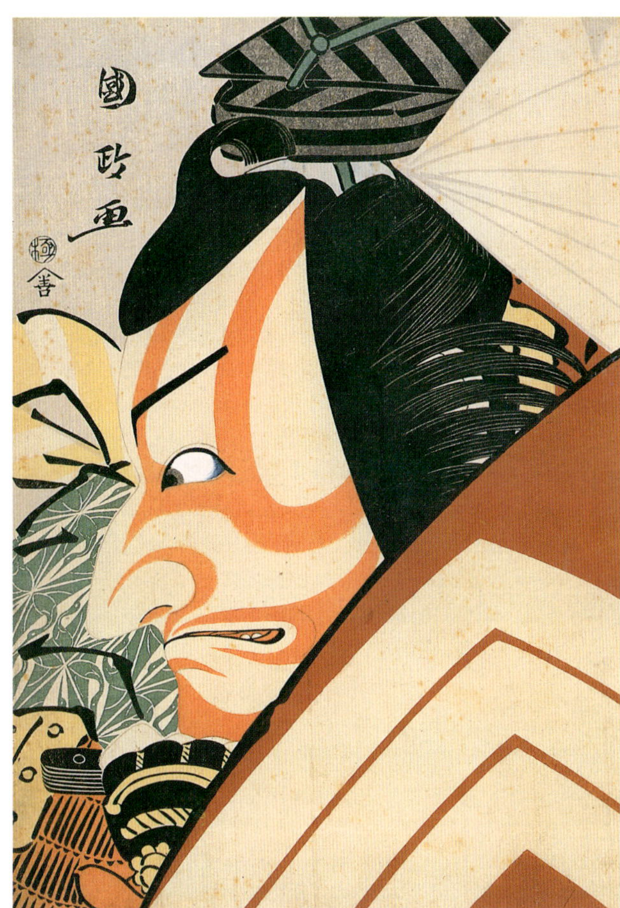

"Kabuki Actor: Ichikawa Danjurō Performing 'Shibaraku' in 1796." Utagawa KUNIMASA (1773–1810). Full-color, *ōban* print. The Tokyo National Museum.

disenfranchised merchant and artisan classes would have generated envy and insubordination among the peasants in the countryside and among the increasingly restless samurai with small entitlements. The government tried to regulate most aspects of popular culture, from fashion to freedom of travel, and periodically tightened the censorship on printed publications. Thus *ukiyo-e* printmaking developed in an environment on the one hand controlled and on the other bursting with creative and commercial possibilites. Something new in style or subject (within the limits set by convention and government regulation) found an avid audience. The development of each new technique in printmaking, including full-color or multiblock printing, can be seen as an attempt to create something new that would circumvent the restrictions.

Historical Background of Color Woodblock Printing

In the late 17th century when publishers began to sell *ukiyo-e* prints, the history of printing in Japan could already be traced back to the 8th century. A few Japanese books, like the luxurious *Saga-bon* of the early 17th century, had been printed using moveable type. Most books, however, were still in 1700, and indeed until the mid-19th century, apparently for reasons of cost, printed by hand, without a press, by rubbing a sheet of paper laid on the inked ridges of a carved woodblock. All printed pictures (including illustrations in the *Saga-bon*) were produced from the same type of single, carved woodblocks as for book texts, in this traditional method that had long been used to replicate Buddhist images or to illustrate scrolls and books of didactic or classic literature. Woodblock printed illustrations were limited to one color: usually black (on white paper), unless pigments were painted in painstakingly by hand. The black was *sumi* ink, a mixture of soot with water, used throughout the orient for painting and writing as well as printing.

The earliest *ukiyo-e* woodblock prints were thus monochromatic, printed only in black. And virtually all the early printed *ukiyo-e*, such as the work of Moronobu, were illustrations for the various types of popular books that began to develop.

Moronobu signed himself not "artist of *ukiyo-e*," but "master of *yamato-e*." Scholars trace the origins of the *ukiyo-e* style to within that central, if nebulous, tradition of artistic expression and theme in Japanese art which is considered "*yamato*" or "Japanese" as opposed to "Chinese style" painting. *Yamato-e* grew out of the Heian courtly aestheticism of the 10th and 11th centuries. Hints of the *ukiyo-e* style can be found in *yamato-e* of the Tosa school and in late 16th and 17th century painted screens of genre subjects. By 1700 important aspects of the style and typical *ukiyo-e* subjects were clearly recognizeable in many of Moronobu's (and other artist's) illustrations.

Human figures (or objects) were done in strong, even outlines. Careful attention went to the realistic details of hairstyles and costumes, but not to a naturalistic depiction of facial features. Moronobu like most *ukiyo-e* artists was uninterested in modeling or shading to indicate volume and recession in space. Instead he concentrated on line and the flat effects of linear patterns. The woodblock medium lent itself to clear outlines filled in with linear patterns, simplified forms, and empty backgrounds, which all continued to be given prominence even after the introduction of color.

From around 1700 *ukiyo-e* artists (or their intrepid publishers) discovered customers for single-sheet woodblock prints that could be sold in series (without text) or alone, often to be hung-up or pasted on an interior panel or pillar, and admired like a painting. Many Edo publishers of popular books thus became at the same time publishers of *ukiyo-e* prints. While publishers in Kamigata, the urban area of modern Osaka and Kyoto, took an early lead in bringing out popular books illustrated in the *ukiyo-e* style, single-sheet printmaking came to be dominated by Edo.

Soon colors were regularly painted by brush on *ukiyo-e* prints. Sugimura Jihei's erotic print series produced in the late 17th century, or full-length depictions of beauties by the Kaigetsudō artists of the opening years of the 18th century are examples of prints with added colors. Torii Kiyonobu (1664–1729) was an early print designer famous for prints with eye-catching orange-red (a pigment called *tan*) and yellow. Among the *ukiyo-e* artists several families appeared which handed down stylistic techniques, commissions, and their names through several generations. These families were really schools since instead of sons talented followers of a master were often allowed to adopt the name. Kiyonobu founded the most prolific and long-lasting—the Torii school—which has specialized in Kabuki theatrical posters and actor prints until the present. Many later Torii school artists designed full-color woodblock prints.

By the 1730's *ukiyo-e* printmakers highlighted hair and details of costume (such as *obi*) by painting in the areas with a dark, glossy black, which

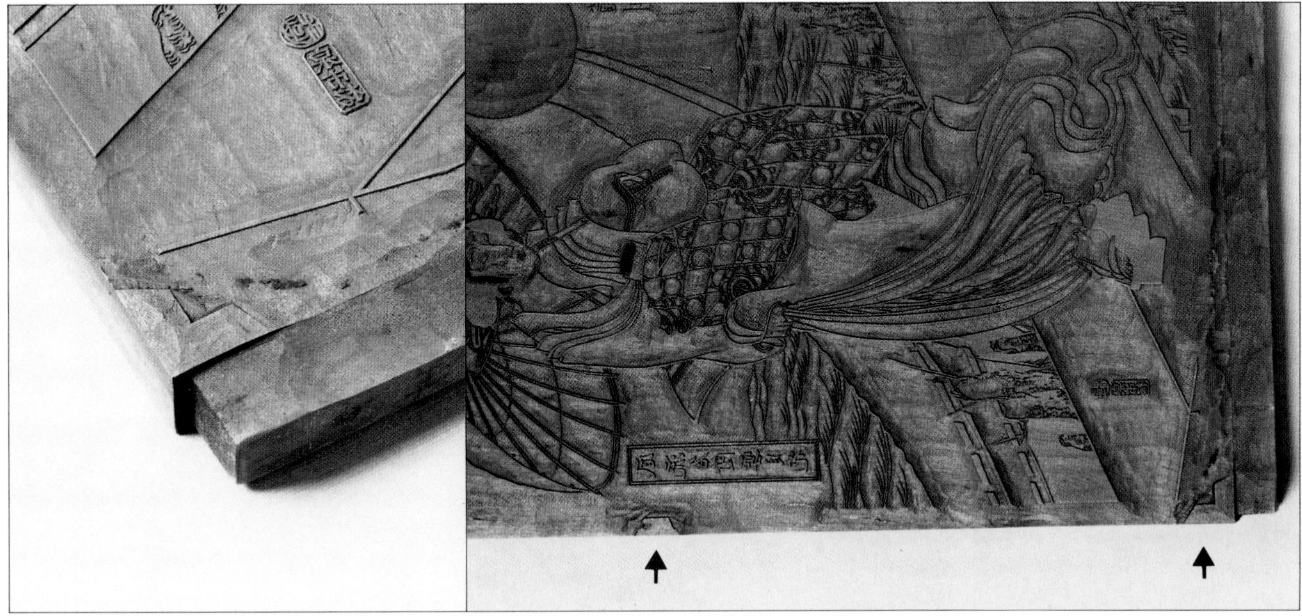

KENTŌ Guide Marks. The printer lays a corner of the paper face-down in the "L" shaped ridge-and-groove (seen here at left and again at lower right) and aligns the sheet with the straight groove (*hikitsuke*) along one side of the woodblock to ensure that each impression prints in register.

resembles lacquer (hence the name *urushi-e* or "lacquer-prints"), made by adding *nikawa* glue to *sumi.* By the 1740's the palette had changed to include a rose-red and a green, or sometimes a yellow. This red was a pigment made from safflowers, or *beni*, giving rise to the term *beni-e* for the type. Ishikawa Toyonobu (1711–85) and the innovative Okumura Masanobu (1686–1764), among others, designed *urushi* and *beni* prints.

The Beginnings of Color Printing

Painting-in areas of a print by hand raised costs and slowed production, and hence limited the number of prints in an edition. Also uniformity of color was hard to obtain.

The major technical problem in printing colors was to align the colored areas neatly within the outlines which are so important to *ukiyo-e* style. Each color requires at least one impression from its own woodblock. Each time the paper is printed brings a risk of blurring and misalignment. The secret of prevention lies in a pair of guide marks known as *kentō*, consistently carved on all the blocks in a set.

One legend suggests *kentō* originated with a blockcarver named Kaneroku. Another record says that Uemura Kichiemon of the print shop Emiya devised the *kentō* in 1744. An idea so simple yet so efficient probably had no single inventor. Chinese had used registration devices for color printing much earlier. Moreover, printed color illustrations for small private editions of poetry anthologies are known to have existed from the 1730's (certainly before 1744). The first printed color *ukiyo-e* prints did appear in the late 1740's. The printed colors on *ukiyo-e* prints of the 1740's and 1750's, however, remained limited to the rose-red and green (with an occasional additional color) of handcolored prints and are still known as *benizuri-e* ("printed *beni-e*").

Full-color Woodblock Printing and *Nishiki-e*

The earliest·extant full-fledged color prints are several picture calendars (*egoyomi*) created by Suzuki Harunobu (1725–70) for the year 1765. Picture calendars had, hidden within their designs, clues that told the number of days in each month, which varied each year according to the old Japanese system. Because they were privately commissioned, these picture calendars are closer to the type of woodblock print called *suri-mono*. These were privately commissioned and circulated announcement prints or prints with designs accompanying the latest verse of poetry groups. *Surimono* employed the most extravagant woodblock printing techniques and materials. They also had a broader range of subject matter than commercial *ukiyo-e* prints that catered to the general public and were subject to greater scrutiny by the censor. The authorities had earlier· banned the commercial publication of calendars, reserving this activity as a government monopoly. This led to a brief period of intense competition in the mid-1760's during which wealthy diletanttes privately commissioned their own picture calendars to hand out to their friends and to poetry cronies at the New Year. Almost immediately, some of the privately commissioned full-color designs by Harunobu (without the calendrical elements) were re-printed in larger, commercial, editions and offered for sale in Edo.

Commercial *ukiyo-e* prints that displayed a complete range of printed colors were soon called *nishiki-e* ("brocade prints"). The name refers to their supposed resemblance to colorful silk brocade. The print, "Snow," by Eizan, used in this book to show the steps in color woodblock printing is a *nishiki-e*. Although the following discussion focuses on making a single-sheet *nishiki-e*, color printmaking techniques are basically the same for full-color book illustrations and *surimono* as well.

Those involved in producing the earliest full-color prints based on Harunobu's designs in 1765 seem to have been conscious of the path-breaking nature of their efforts, because the calendar prints carry the names of the master blockcarver and printer along with Harunobu's. This acknowledgement of others besides the artist virtually never appears on *nishiki-e*. That is, until the closing years of the Edo period (the mid-19th century), when it became the custom for the blockcarver's name, occasionally accompanied by the printer's name, to appear in an *ukiyo-e* print, or printed just outside the composition in the margin.

Thus, behind the major artists who designed the full-color *ukiyo-e* prints that are now so famous worked, usually annonymously, blockcarvers and printers, as well as the truly unknown craftspeople responsible for preparing the blocks, tools, or paper. The publisher also played an indispensible role in choosing subjects, overseeing the project and ensuring sales. Full-color woodblock printmaking involved the efforts of a team.

"Young Girl in a Summer Shower" (*Egoyomi*), 1765. Suzuki HARUNOBU.
Full-color, *chūban* print. The Art Institute of Chicago.

This earliest full-color print was designed as a picture calendar. The calendrical elements can be found disguised amid the patterns on *obi* and robe hung out to dry.

The name at mid-left: Hakusei *kō* (and seal: "*Shokoku sei'in*") indicates the patron, Hakusei, a *kyōka* poet and Edo dilettante who commissioned the work. Written at lower right (seen in detail below) are the names of artist, Suzuki HARUNOBU, blockcarver, Endō Goryoku, and printer, Yumoto Kōshi. Harunobu is listed with the same title-*kō* ("artisan") as the other two. This leveling usage (found more often in illustrated books than on prints) suggests that the contributions of the now forgotten carver and printer were considered nearly equal with that of the artist designer.

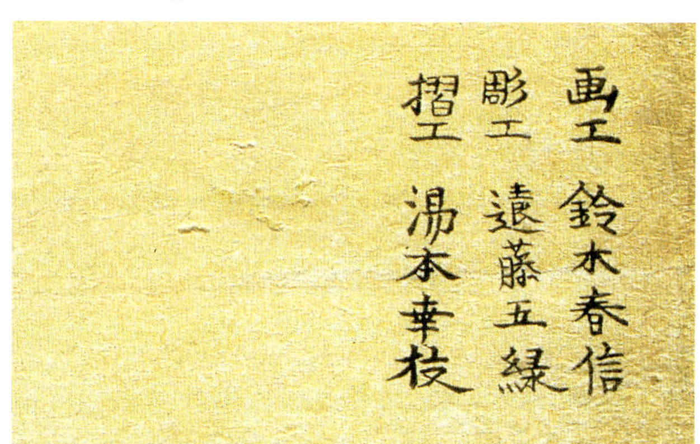

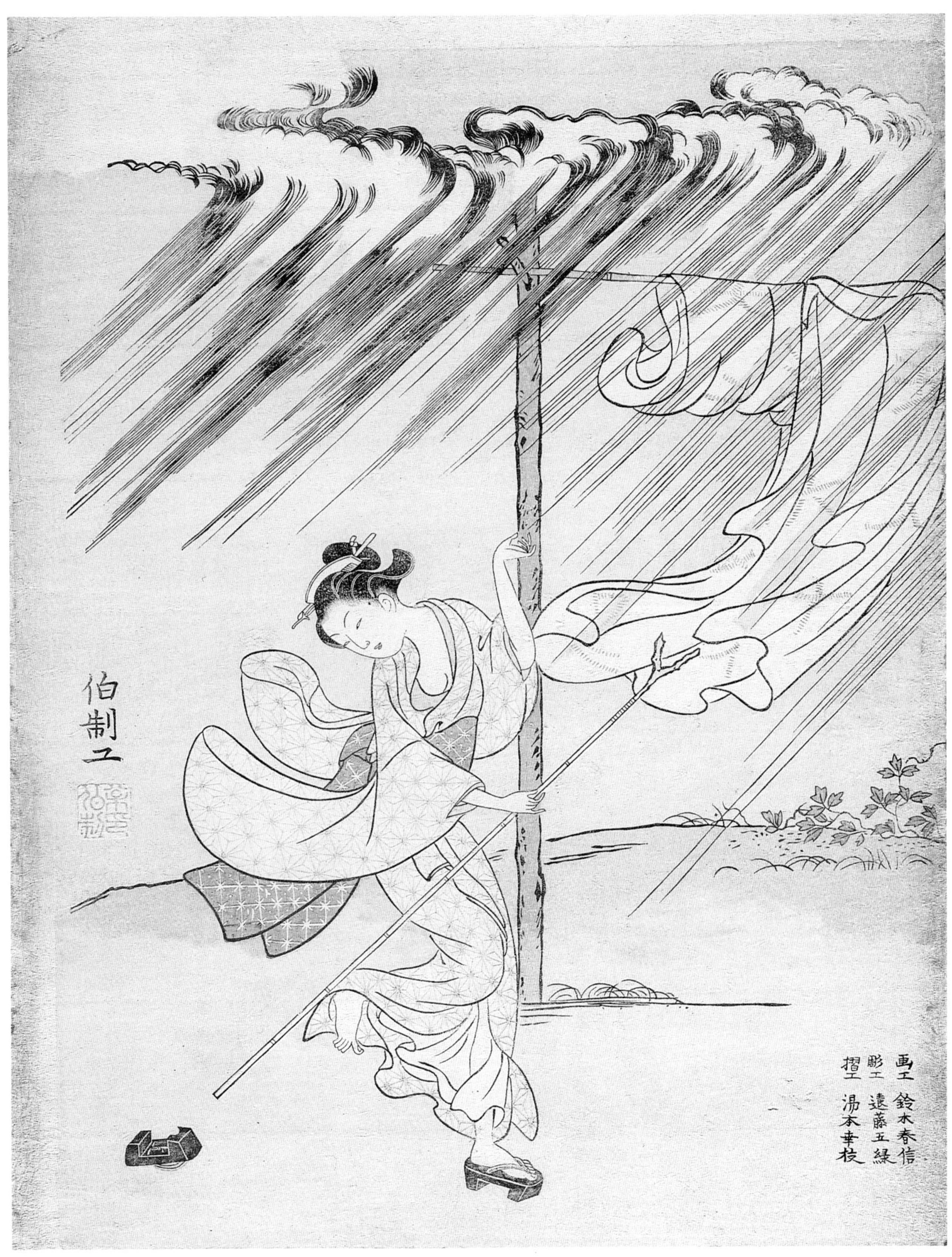
伯制工
画工　鈴木春信
彫工　遠藤五緑
摺工　湯本幸枝

Despite that caveat, the direction full-color printmaking took after 1765 can be seen in a brief summary of the most important artists who designed prints. What is here little more than a list of names provided as a quick reference may be supplemented by any of the excellent and thoroughly illustrated histories of *ukiyo-e*.

Harunobu was a master at bringing an inner balance and elegance to his compositions. His diminuative female beauties are characteristic of his style. Along with Harunobu, Isoda Koryūsai (active c.1763–85), Katsukawa Shunshō (1726–92) famous for his actor prints, and Ippitsusai Bunchō (active until around 1770) by exploiting the new possiblities of the full-color print helped usher in an exciting era.

Torii Kiyonaga (1752–1815) in the 1780's made a name for himself with his depictions of tall, statuesque beauties and their dandies. Several of his most famous prints show scenes of pleasures set along the river banks of Edo. At this time, the large size *ōban* format, which could be expanded into diptychs and triptychs to add further compositional interest, became standard for *nishiki-e*.

Probably the best known full-color print designer is Kitagawa Utamaro (1753–1806). The work of Utamaro along with that of Tōshūsai Sharaku (active for only one year; 1794) made the 1790's the golden age of *nishiki-e*. The two aimed for a psychological realism often closer to true portraiture than other *ukiyo-e* artists. Their designs show energy and daring. Particularly with the encouragement of publisher Tsutaya

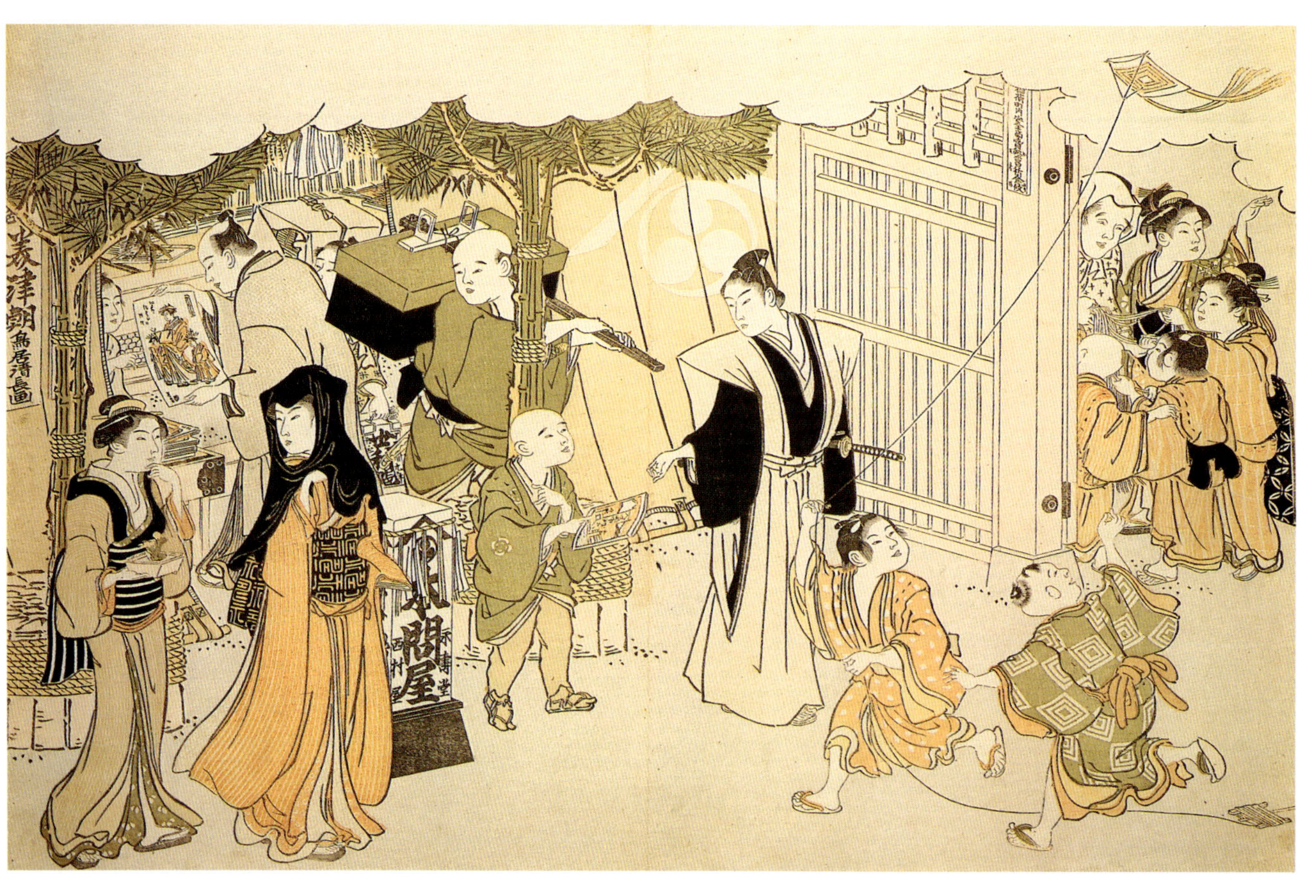

From "Morning of the New Year in Color" (*Saishiki mitsu no asa*), 1787. Torii KIYONAGA. Book published by Nishimuraya Yohachi. At New Year's, children fly a kite in front of the Edo book and print publisher, Nishimuraya (written on the sign post). At left is a placard self-advertising the book. A customer inspects a new courtesan print (by Kiyonaga?). At center what seems to be a roving bookseller prepares to set out, and a young shop-clerk purveys this book, or perhaps another new title. Most illustrated popular fiction and many prints first went on sale at the New Year's season.
The Boston Museum of Fine Arts.

Jūsaburō (1750–97), they, and the craftsmen who produced the prints, were technical innovators. Their prints were among the first to use irridescent mica backgrounds. Utamaro also created designs which called forth the greatest of carving and printing skills in the depictions of human figures seen through translucent fabrics and mesh. Another technical *tour de force* were Utamaro's compositions printed on both sides of the paper sheet so as to show, for example, a beautiful woman in full-face on the front and then her back on the reverse. Little is known about Sharaku's family background or with whom he studied. Some say he was a Kamigata man, possibly an actor. His brief one-year career as a print designer has left us a series of striking portraits of actors.

Two other important print designers active at

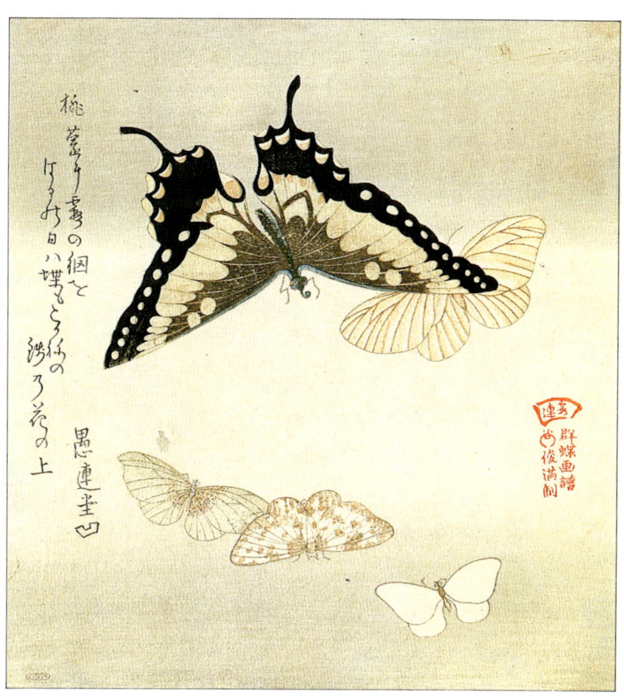

"Collection of Butterflies" (*Gunchō gafū*).
Kubota SHUNMAN.
Surimono, shikishi page with *kyōka* poetry.
The Tokyo National Museum.

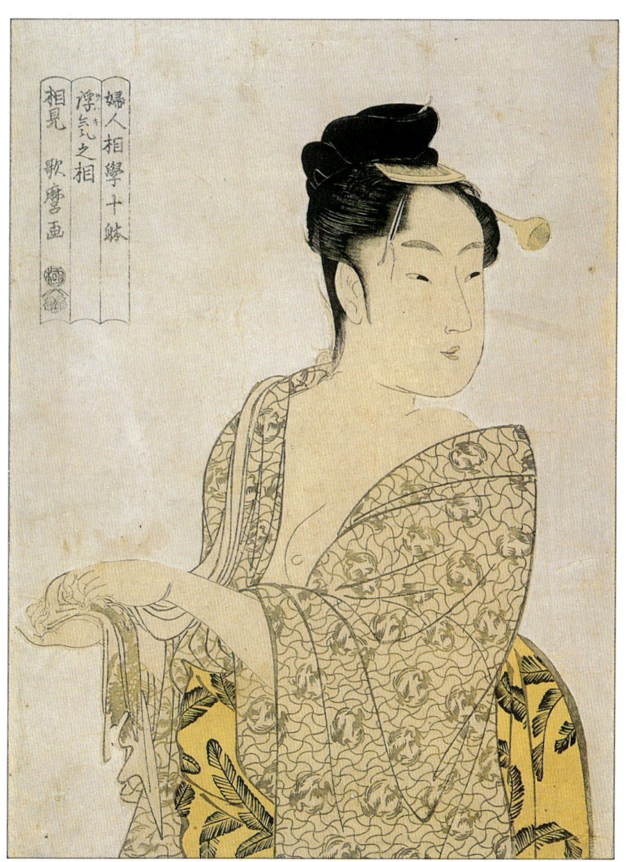

"The Passionate Type" (*Uwaki no so*) from the series, "Ten Physiognomic Aspects of Women," ca 1791.
Kitagawa UTAMARO.
Full-color, *ōban* print with mica. The Tokyo National Museum.

the turn of the century and inspiring many followers were Chōbunsai Eishi (1756–1829), known for his elegant designs of slender beautiful women, and Utagawa Toyokuni (1769–1825), famous for his powerful actor prints. Katsukawa Shun'ei (1768–1819) followed his teacher, Shunshō, and produced many fine actor and wrestler prints.

The period from around 1790 until the 1830's witnessed the peak in *surimono* popularity. These prints were privately commissioned by members of Edo poetry (*kyōka*) groups. Katsushika Hokusai (1760–1849), Totoya Hokkei (1780–1850), Gakutei (1786?–1868), and Kubota Shunman (1757–1820) deserve mention as the great colorists of *surimono*.

While *surimono* for a limited group of connoisseurs reached new design and technical heights, the quality of the subjects and execution of commercial *ukiyo-e* prints overall declined. The power of the shogunal government weakened and as the arbitrary controls on popular expression briefly tightened then loosened, the collective imagination seemed pushed to increasing extremes. The number of Edo print publishers rose dramatically. Less expensive *ukiyo-e* prints in ever greater numbers reached a wider, less discriminating audience. The first half of the 19th century is often called the period of "decadence" in *ukiyo-e*, yet it produced undeniable masterpieces among full-color prints.

Hokusai, with the first in his series "Thirty-six Views of Mt. Fuji" in 1823, introduced the commercial landscape print for the mass audience. Printmakers turned to landscape themes at a time of tightened government restrictions. Hokusai fully exploited a certain amount of simplification, the bold forms, imposed by the woodblock medium. His work also shows that Japanese artists had by now internalized aspects of European style such as one-point perspective techniques. Growing out of the creative leeway allowed in his designs for *surimono* and spurred by restrictions on contemporaneous subject matter, Hokusai also produced prints of "birds and flowers", subjects rarely encountered before in *ukiyo-e*.

Andō Hiroshige's (1797–1858) great work in landscape *nishiki-e* started in the 1830's with his series "Fifty-three Stations on the Tōkaidō". His landscape prints beautifully capture a range of atmospheric phenomena. Hiroshige had studied under the Utagawa school, the dominant school of the early 19th century. Utagawa artists had been active since the time of Toyokuni and the *uki-e* "perspective-landscapes" of Utagawa Toyoharu (1735–1814). Utagawa Kuniyoshi (1797–1861) is famous for decadent beauties and action-packed, imaginative scenes derived from history and legend. His rival in the school, Kunisada (1786–1864), took actors as the subjects of his most com-

"View on a Fine, Breezy Day," from the series, "Thirty-six Views of Mt. Fuji," ca 1830.
Katsushika HOKUSAI. Full-color, *ōban* print. The Tokyo National Museum.

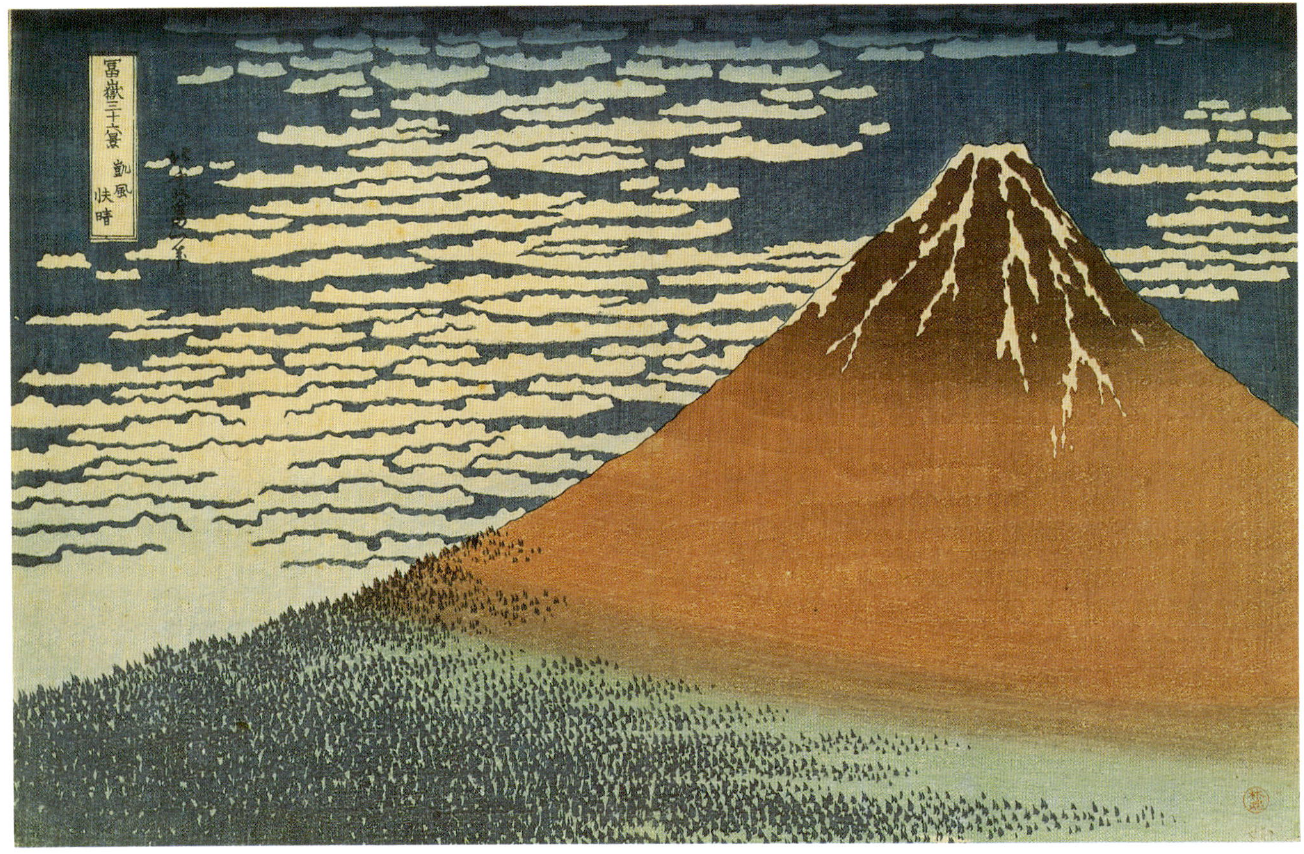

pelling prints.

Two other artists of the time who managed to make a name outside of the Utagawa school were Keisai Eisen (1790–1848) and Kikukawa Eizan (1787–1867). Eisen, who studied under the Kanō school and later Eizan, was noted for his slightly lascivious depictions of women and for landscapes.

A full-color print of a beauty, "Snow", by Eizan, dating from about 1810, has been chosen as a representative example of the full-color woodblock process for this book. Eizan's biography emphasizes his precociousness. He studied the Kanō tradition under his father and then took the Shijō school painter Suzuki Nanrei (1775–1844) for a teacher. As a print designer he was influenced by Utamaro. Probably through his friendship with Hokkei, the important *surimono* artist and follower of Hokusai, Eizan was also influenced by Hokusai's style. His best known works are of beauties reminiscent of the late Utamaro and he is also known for compositions featuring women and children and for actor prints, some interesting, some rather uninspired. He founded the Kikugawa school, but retired from printmaking around 1830, and his last years were passed in obscurity.

The Meiji Restoration in 1868 accomplished the opening of Japan to the west and set the country rushing along the path of modernization and industrialization. The *ukiyo-e* tradition, no longer a dominent artistic style, continued in the work of artists like Toyohara Kunichika (1835–1900). Tsukioka Yoshitoshi (1839–92) brought a new sensibility to color woodblock printmaking, while Kobayashi Kiyochika (1847–1915) incorporated new—to Japanese eyes—western stylistic techniques. Contacts with foreigners, current events, new inventions, technical developments and fashions that were rapidly changing the face of the city, became the subjects for full-color woodblock prints.

To most intents and purposes the 20th century ushered in the end of *ukiyo-e* as an independent or creative force. The traditional techniques of woodblock carving and printing (and some elements of artistic style the methods encouraged) continued to be found in the prints of a few

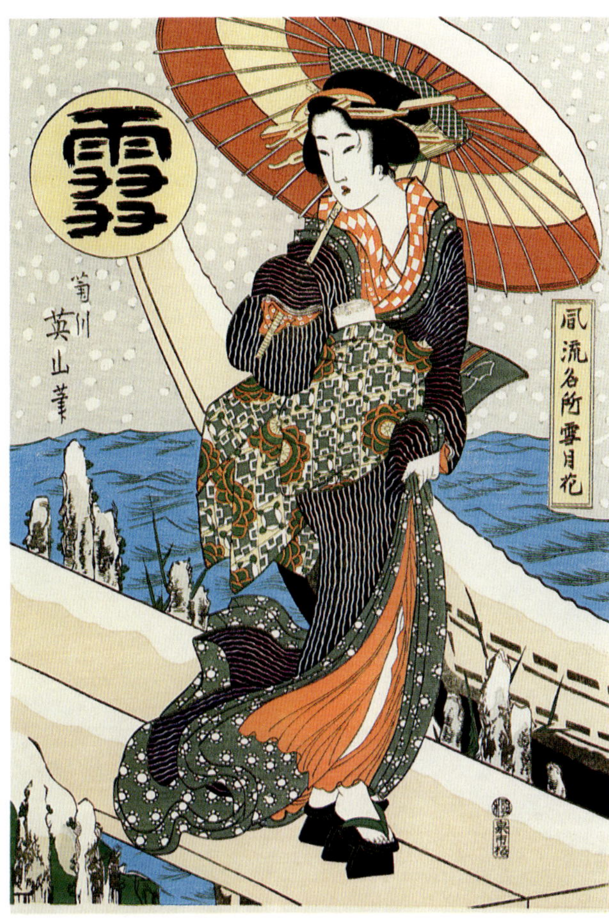

"Snow," from a triptych "Fashionable, Famous Sites: Snow, Moon, and Blossoms" (*Furyū meisho setsugekka*), ca 1810. Kikukawa EIZAN.
Full-color, *ōban* print. Published by Izumi Ichibei.

Each of the three prints in the triptych depicts a beautiful modern woman at a popular assignation spot, as a parody (*mitate*) of the old landscape painting theme of snow, moon, and cherry blossoms. Here the play on an ancient subject is emphasized by the use of an archaic form of the character for "snow" in the large circle at left. The setting probably depicts the boat landing at Fukagawa, in Edo. The geisha assumes a rather risque pose as the cold wind blows open her kimono. A certain brittleness given her facial features and prominence of undainty feet are typical of 19th century *ukiyo-e* beauties. This is a modern reproduction, used throughout this book to illustrate the printmaking process.

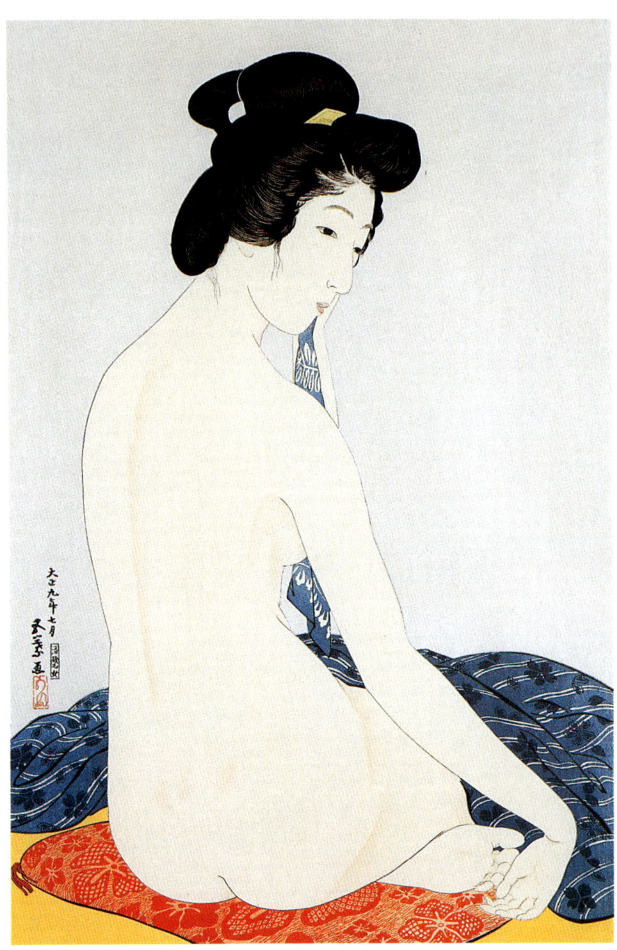

"Nude."
Itoh Shinsui.
Full-color woodblock print.   Private collection.

modern Japanese artists.   Hashiguchi Goyō (1880?–1921), considered one of the last *ukiyo-e* artists, and Ito Shinsui (1889–1972) relied on the traditional division of labor between artist and craftsmen to produce woodblock prints, mainly of beautiful women.   But the most original woodblock prints, like those of Onchi Kōshiro (1891–1955) done in abstract style, were produced by artists influenced by the western 20th-century ideal of the artist as his own printmaker.   When artists took over the entire printmaking process they usually abandoned many of the complicated and time-consuming full-color woodblock techniques.

Making a Full-Color Woodblock Print

The Paper Used for Woodblock Prints

Japanese traditional paper is called *washi* not as still sometimes heard "rice paper". *Washi* has nothing to do with rice, unless one counts tiny amounts of rice-starch paste sometimes used for sizing. Rather it is made from various types of plant fibers. These long fibers make a stronger, more supple paper than wood chips used for modern paper in the west. The major types of *washi* are differentiated by the plants used to make each variety. Most *ukiyo-e* color woodblock prints were printed on *washi* made primarily from fibers of the paper mulberry, or *kōzo* (*Broussonetia kajinoki*).

The process for making *kōzo* paper, which can still be seen today in a few places such as Otaki, in Fukui prefecture (old Eichizen province), follows the traditional methods of the Edo period. As with other skills involved in the print-making process, certain details we see today may have changed since the 19th century. Earlier written records which would make a comparison possible do not appear to exist.

In the Edo period peasants engaged in paper production during the cool months when their farm and forestry tasks were less pressing. At least from the mid-18th century papermaking had come to thrive as an arduous cottage industry that was often the sole source of income for villages in remote or mountainous areas unsuited for rice cultivation.

After harvesting the paper mulberry, because of regular cutting more a woody bush with thin stems than a tree, the papermaker stripped off the dark outer bark. Long soaking or sometimes steaming the bundles of stems facilitated this laborious first step. Then the whitish inner fibers were boiled, and all bits of bark or debris carefully picked out. The long fibers were then pounded to soften and were further washed.

Finally, with the addition of *tororo-aoi* starch, a pulpy solution was readied. The papermaker skillfully scooped out an appropriate amount of this into a long, hand-held tray with its bottom lined in a bamboo-slat screen. A constant rocking motion deposited the fibers evenly over the

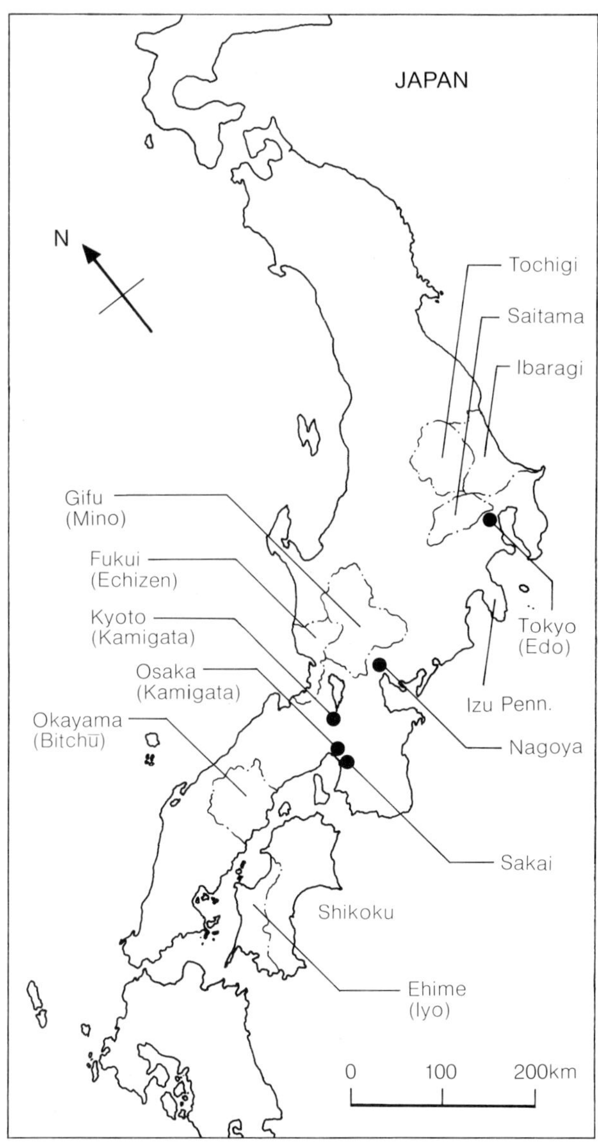

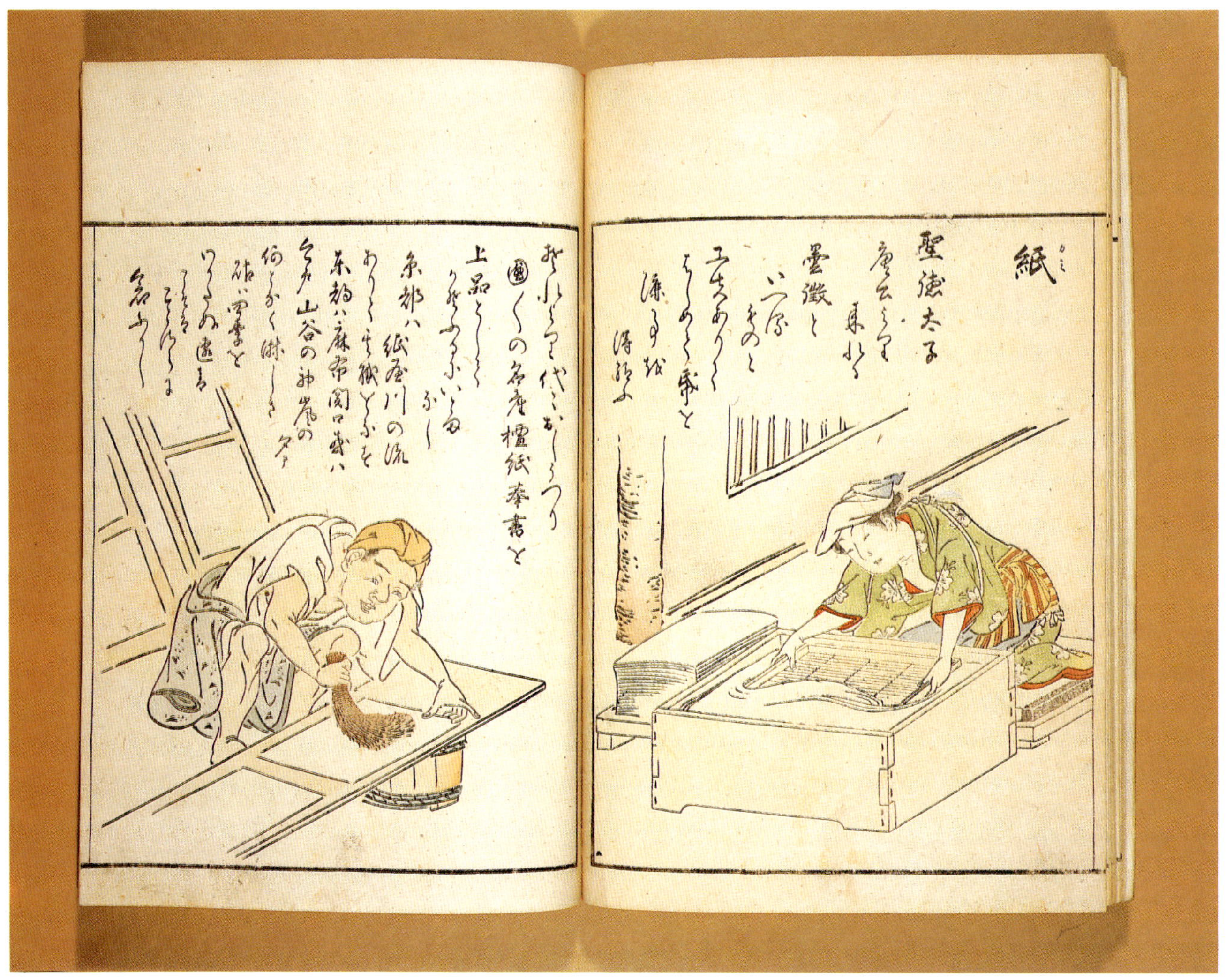

Making Paper (*washi*). At right, a woman artisan scoops up pulpy liquid into a hand-held tray with bamboo screen at bottom. Another artisan then brushes each damp sheet to prevent wrinkles as they are laid out on boards to dry. Illustration by Kanō school artist in "Craftspeople at Work, Painted in Color" (*Saiga shokunin burui*), early 19th c. National Diet Library.

screen while the water drained through. The wet sheet was peeled off, and then (after a number had been produced) each sheet was transferred from the pile to be stretched on a board and set out in the sun to dry. The slat marks of the screen remain visible in the semi-translucent finished sheets of paper used for prints. The size of the tray-screen, which varied somewhat from place to place but was ultimately limited by the artisan's armspan, determined the size of the sheets of paper.

Packages of untrimmed finished paper were wrapped in an outer covering of straw-matting and tied with braid to be carried out of the vil-

lages by backpack or horse. Ships often transported the paper from the castle towns of the feudal domains to wholesaler's warehouses in Edo or Sakai (Osaka). Wholesalers sold the paper to publishers who in turn commissioned and supplied the printers.

In terms of quanity, most full-color woodblock prints (*nishiki-e*) were printed on *kōzo* paper called *masa*. *Masa* is a smooth grain, lightweight paper. Off-white in color, it is semi-translucent when held up to the light. Sometimes *masa* may contain a small amount of other fibers besides *kōzo*. The name *masa* was generically applied to all but the highest grades of *kōzo* paper which were called *hōsho.* *Hōsho* was the paper used for most documents during the Edo period, and the term derived from an original meaning of "official paper for government decrees." The terms *masa* and *hōsho* alone or in combinations, for example with local place names of production, were applied to a spectrum of papers of only slightly different quality and sheet size. For example, records say that *iyo-masa* replaced by the 1830's *iyo-bōsho* as a widely used paper for *nishiki-e.* This type of record is sometimes cited as documentary evidence for the noted decline in paper quality used for *nishiki-e* in the 19th century. Another account says that *iyo-bōsho* was just another name for *masa.* In any case, the old province of Iyo, now Ehime prefecture in Shikoku, seems to have been a major source of paper for *nishiki-e.* On the other hand, Bitchū (Okayama) and especially Eichizen (Fukui) are regarded as the chief production areas of the fine quality *hōsho* paper. Thicker, whiter, more supple and expensive than ordinary *masa* paper, *hōsho* was used for special *nishiki-e* (including many of the now regarded masterpieces of the late 18th century). *Hōsho* was routinely used for the privately commissioned and superbly printed *surimono.* Easily burnished, *hōsho* readily picked up gauffrage.

Paper produced for color woodblock prints from the mid-19th century in the modern Tokyo area at Hodogaya and Otowa was called *jimasa.* The inferior quality of this paper may have helped to give *masa* its present reputation for low quality. Craftsmen producing traditional full-color woodblock prints today use exclusively *hōsho* paper, made of 100% *kōzo* fibers, that only one or two families in Fukui still make.

An added complication to understanding the types and terminology for the paper of Edo period and 19th century full-color woodblock prints comes from the use of the same terms *masa* and *hōsho* to indicate size as well as type of paper. Thus today printers may still say "*masa-ban*" for a standard large-sheet size of *hōsho* paper.

Some reference books and catalogues give print sizes in the traditional terms (such as *ōban* or *chūban*) based on multiples cut from the old standard sheet sizes. Although confusing because the "standard" varied somewhat, this can be a handy

Commonly Encountered Paper Sizes for Full-color Woodblock Prints

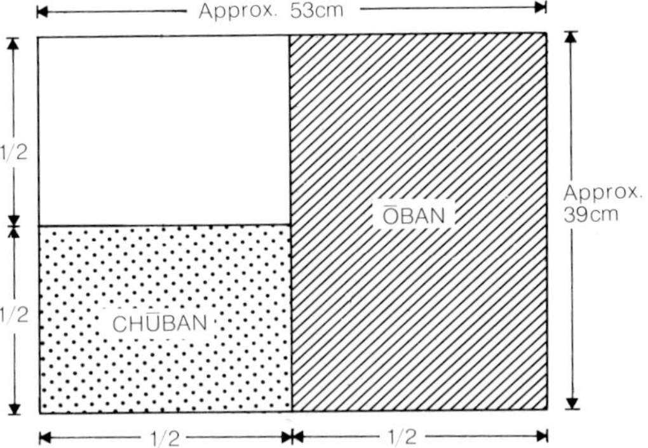

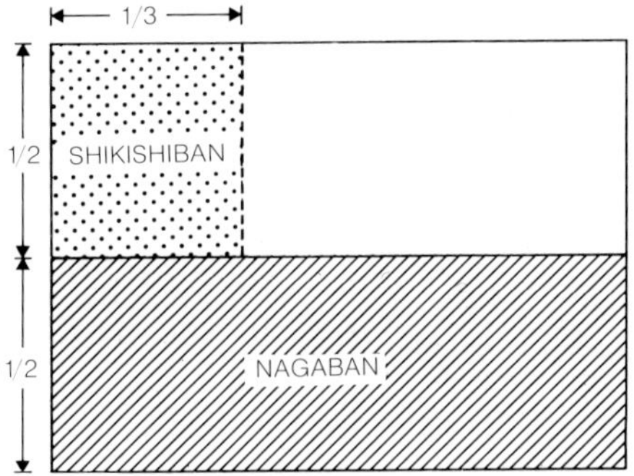

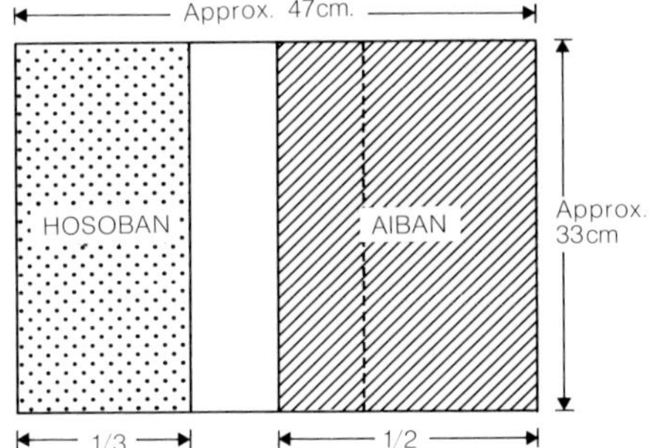

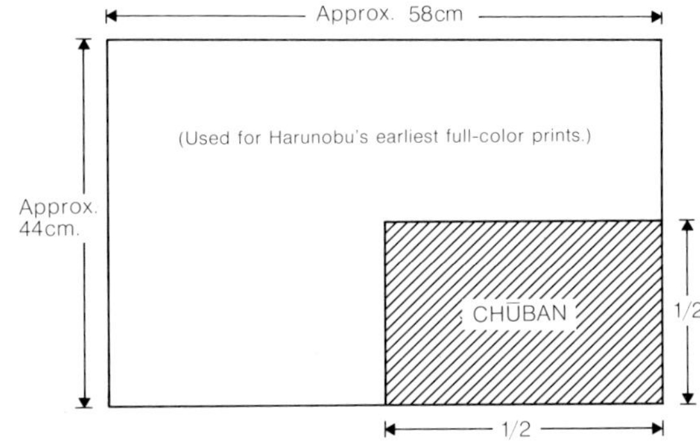

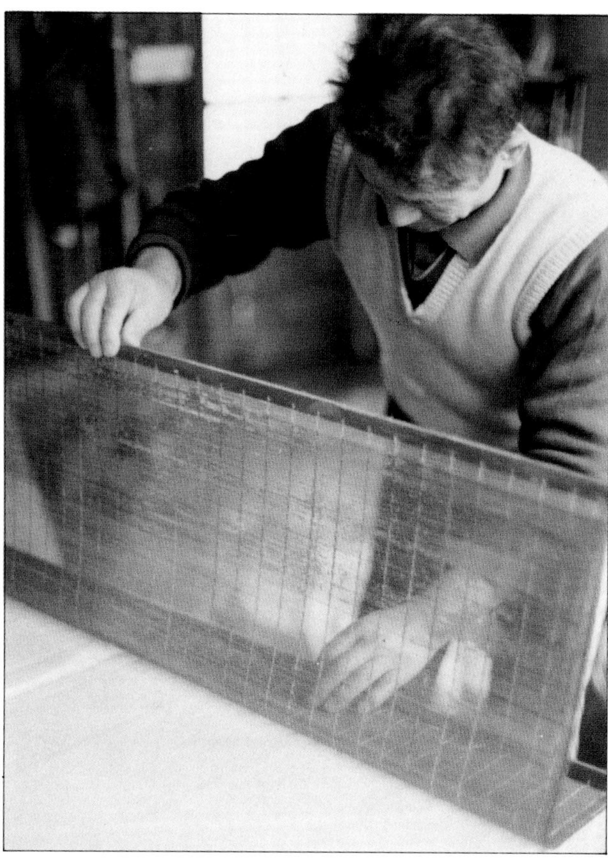

A modern papermaker removes the bamboo-slat screen as he lays a still wet sheet of just-made *washi* in the pile. The faint marks of the screen (slats and filament) remain in the finished paper used for woodblock prints.

way of referring to prints. A sheet (called *ōbōsho* or "large *hōsho*") when cut in half gave the most common format size of *nishiki-e*: the large format, or *ōban*, size of approximately 10 × 15in or 39 × 26cm. This *ōban* size was often then combined in multiples to give diptychs and triptychs. Each print in such a series could stand independently, laid together, however, they created a unified larger composition. Each print was on a separate sheet and thus called for a separate set of woodblocks. Other multiples (six, nine, etc.) based on the *ōban* (and to a lesser extent other format sizes) are also found. Besides *ōban*, the other most widely encountered format sizes for full-color woodblock prints are summarized in the chart.

There are other types of *washi* encountered when examining or discussing woodblock prints. A heavier variety of *mino* paper, produced in the old Mino area (now in Gifu prefecture), was used for prints before the development of full-color printing (that is before the 1760's). It continued to be important in full-color printmaking as lightweight *mino* paper was often used for the master drawing by the artist and for trial prints. *Gampi*, another thin, crisp paper produced in Gifu (and elsewhere) took its name from *gampi* (*Diplomorpha sikokiana* Honda or *Wikstroemia sikokiana*) fibers. This also was used (after an application of sizing) for the master drawing or its copy. *Torinoko*, a heavier and lustrous paper with one side a smooth surface and the other side a finely pitted "eggshell" surface, was usually made from the fibers of *gampi* or from a mixture of *gampi* with *mitsumata* (*Edgeworthia papyrifera*). Eichizen was famous for its production. Renowned as a calligraphy paper, it was rarely used for woodblock prints, except special printed albums, such as Utamaro's *Gifts of the Ebb Tide*. Modern, *shin* (new) *torinoko* is a similar, machine-made paper used today mostly for lithographs and etchings.

A paper called *nishinouchi*, produced in Ibaragi and Tochigi prefectures (other places made similar paper), was not used extensively for *nishiki-e* during the Edo period, but was often employed for prints and Edo-print copies produced in the late 19th and early 20th centuries. *Hosokawa*, one of the many tough (mainly *kōzo* fiber) papers used mostly for *shōji* interior panels, is still produced in Saitama prefecture, not far from Tokyo, where visitors are welcome to observe traditional *washi* making. *Gasenshi* is a thin paper (produced originally in China with later Japanese versions) used for backing or repairing prints.

The Artist's Master Design

As the first step in making a full-color woodblock print the artist produced a design, painted in all black outlines on thin, *mino* or *gampi* paper. The artist worked under the coordination of the publisher, who often suggested subject matter, and who would supervise the whole printmaking process. The publishing process for illustrated popular books was similar but I concentrate below on the making of a *nishiki-e* in Edo.

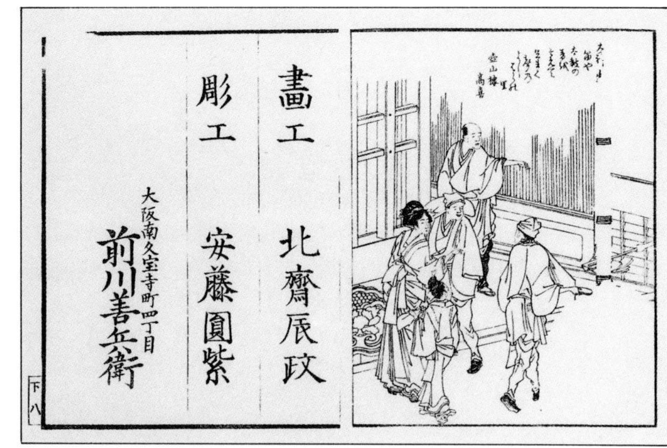

The Publisher

The publisher's choice of artist and craftsmen and his selection of a composition that would sell, yet not offend the authorities, reflected his managerial abilities and his acumen. Attrition in the business was high. Hundreds of names, if not much more, are known of publishers (*hanmoto*) of popular fiction and prints in Edo. To a lesser extent the publishers of popular fiction (not many prints) are known in Kyoto-Osaka, and a smaller number of publisher's names are known in cities like Nagoya. From 1721 the publisher's name and address, as well as the name of illustrator were required on the end-page of all illustrated commercial books. While the regulations were less specific for single-sheet prints, nearly all *nishiki-e* carry, along with the artist's signature, the abbreviated symbol—some now unidentifiable—representing the publisher's mark.

During most of the years of *nishiki-e* publication (1791–1874), if the publisher liked a design, before sending it to the blockcarver, he first had to submit it for the censor's approval. The Edo censor was in fact selected in rotation from among the publishers of popular fiction and prints themselves, except for a brief period (1842–58) when city government officials took charge. The Shogun from early in the 17th century banned publi-

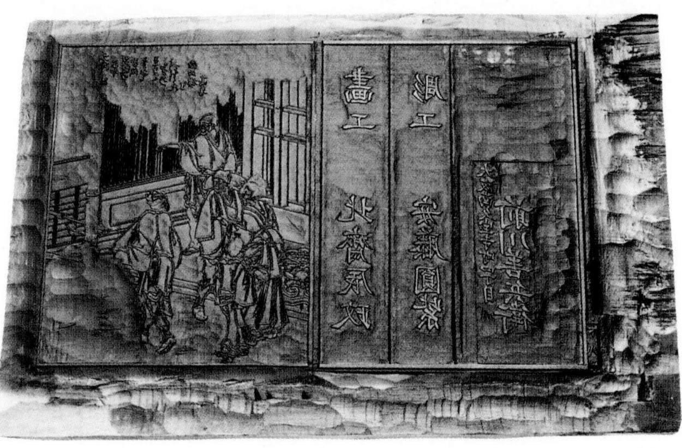

Keyblock print and extant woodblock for the last full-color illustration, "Yoshiwara" and end-page of the book, "A Look Along Both Banks of the River Sumida" (*E-hon Sumidagawa ryōgan ichiran*), illustrated by Hokusai.

First published in 1816, this block is a recarving for a later, 19th century edition. For the end-page, after the names of the artist, HOKUSAI Tatsumasa, and blockcarver, Andō Enshi, the Osaka publisher, Maekawa Zenbei, has had his name and address inserted into the woodblock. The Boston Museum of Fine Arts (courtesy of TBS).

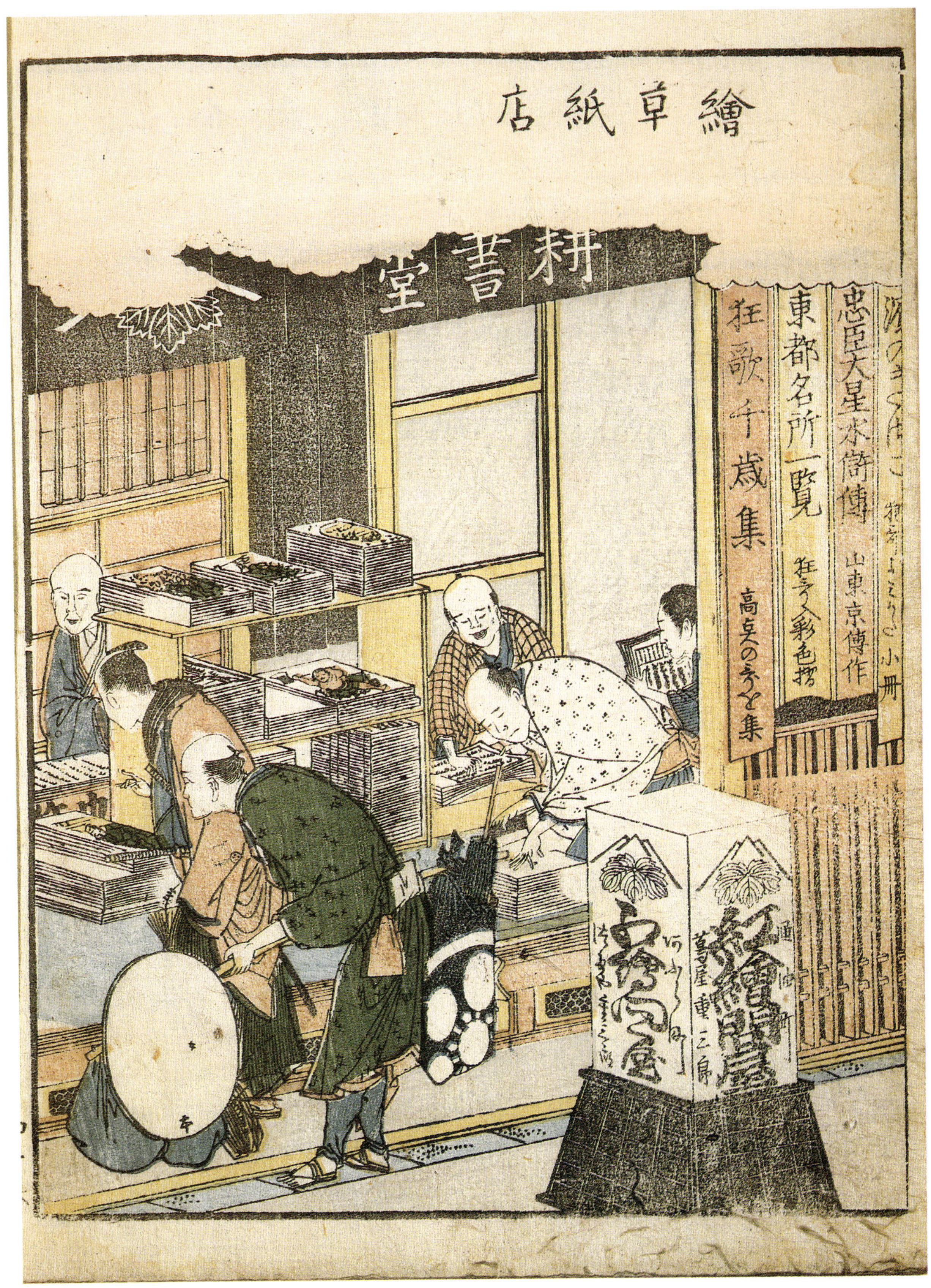
繪草紙店
耕書堂
狂歌千歳集
高㚑のや〱集
東都名所一覧
忠臣大星水滸傳
山東京傳作
繪本
吉原

cation of any sentiments not in line with the government and Confucian-based social order. No members of the samurai elite could be depicted. Regulations were then periodically tightened to include prohibitions on sexually explicit depictions, on references to any contemporary events, even involving townspeople, and on designs too suggestive of fashionableness or ostentation. In a last ditch effort to shore up power and control social unrest, the Tempo reforms of 1842 briefly prohibited even the mainstays of *ukiyo-e* subject matter: actors, courtesans and geisha.

A censor's seal of approval was stamped on the artist's design if it met the criteria. A round "*kiwame*" ("thoroughly", meaning "thoroughly checked") appears often in combination with seals of appropriate date symbols or the censor's name(s). After 1853 it was replaced by "*aratame*" ("examined"); although during the period 1842– 58 Edo officals routinely only used their name seals. The blockcarver faithfully carved the seal impressions into the woodblock with the rest of the composition of the master drawing. Thus they appear on every print in a commercial edition after 1791; and, today, can be useful clues in deciding the year, or even month, of publication.

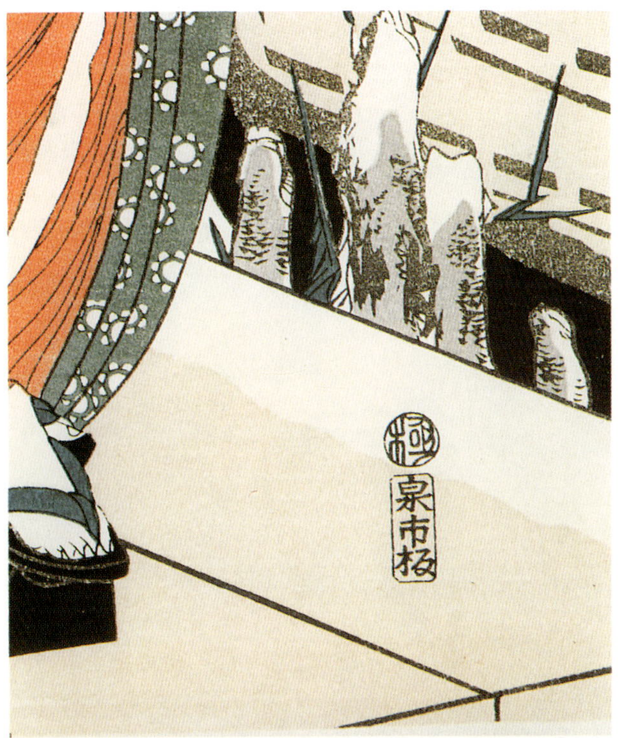

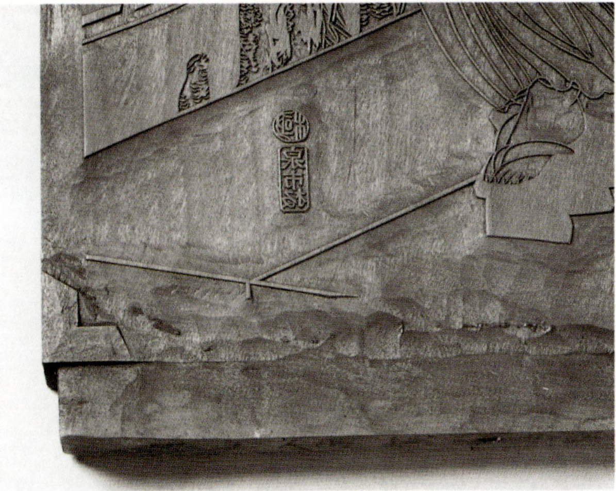

Typical round *kiwame* ("thoroughly checked") censor's seal impression shown as printed and (below) carved in the keyblock above the publisher's mark, "*Izumi-ichihan*," meaning the publisher Izumi Ichibei. The censor's seals, although most often added (as here) near other writing or cartouches, sometimes were placed outside the composition in the margin and eventually were lost through later damage or trimming of the print.

"Publisher Tsutaya's Shop-front" (*Ezōshi-ten*), illustration by Hokusai in the book, "Pleasures of the East[ern Capital]" (*Azuma asobi*), first published in 1801. Courtesy of TBS.

Woodblock prints are offered for sale, stacked in piles. The distinctive shop logo (virtually the same as the publisher's mark found on prints) with ivy leaf appears on *noren* curtain (at left) and on the sign-post ("*Beni-e* Wholesaler"). Men in travel gear, perhaps tourist customers up from the provinces, or more likely, roving middle-men booksellers, haggle with the manager, Jūzaburō, (or his heir since Jūzaburō I had died in 1797) who sits at left. Placards advertise newly published illustrated books.

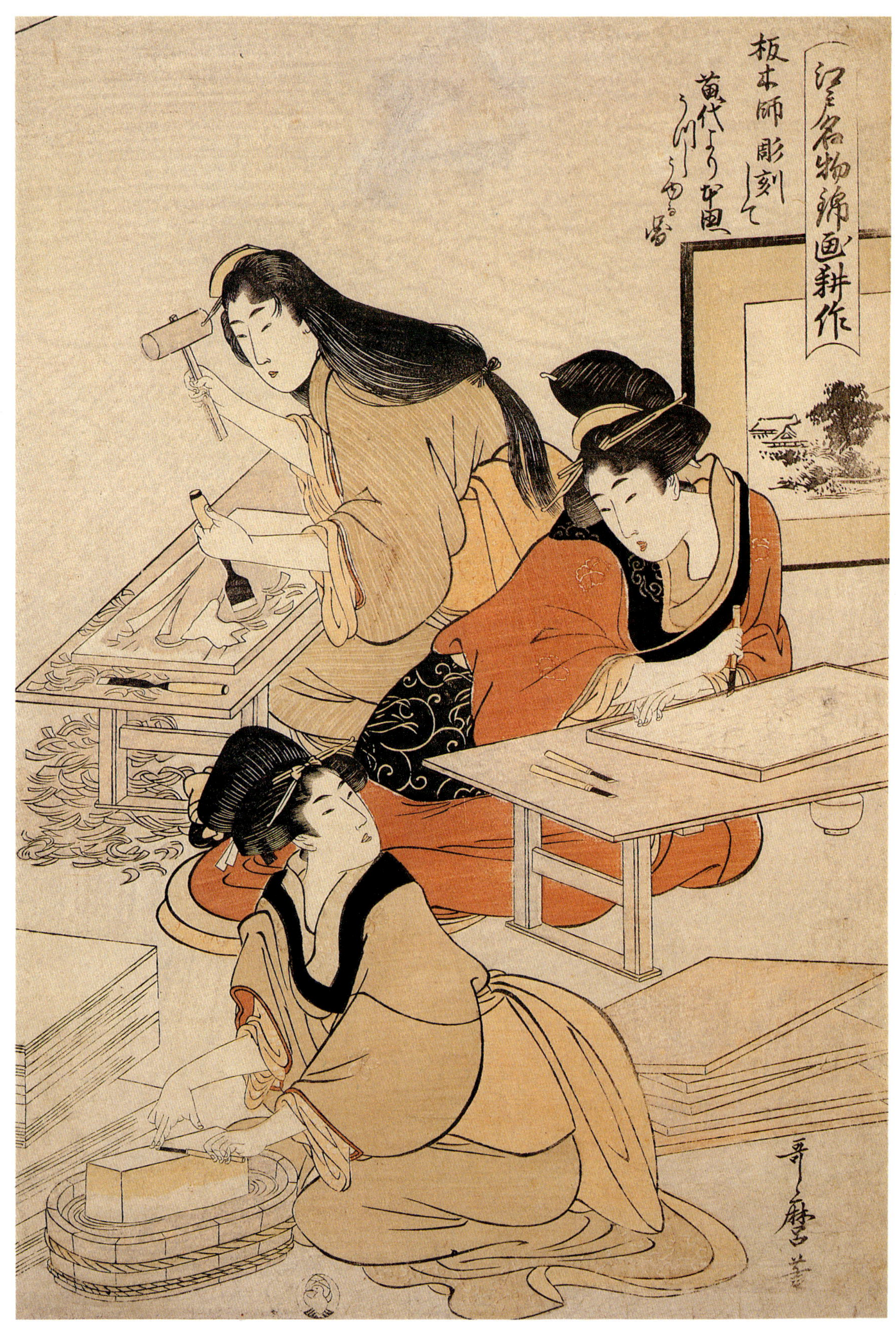

江戸名物錦画耕作
板元師彫刻して
黄代より草画
うつし所す當
歌麿筆

The Woodblock Carver

The publisher sent the approved artist's design to the blockcarver's workshop. It typically comprised the master-carver and his family, live-in apprentices, and assistants, some of whom were hired only for big jobs. A 1791 record lists five blockcarver associations located at Nihonbashi, Asakusa, Shimotani, Bakurōchō, and Yamanote which are areas in and around the northern section of modern Tokyo which is still known for publishing activities. Some writers prefer to call the blockcarvers "engravers".

Details about the blockcarver's profession in the early years of *nishiki-e* (particularly before the last decades of the 18th century) are obscure. Once full-color printmaking was established, some blockcarvers seem to have specialized in *nishiki-e* woodblocks, while others exclusively carved lettering for book-texts. Such specialization would seem a logical development as complicated full-color designs requiring special carving techniques evolved. However, little distinguishes the basic carving of a brushstroke for a calligraphic line from an outline for an *ukiyo-e* figure. Anecdotes by contemporary blockcarvers about "the old days" suggest that under the master-apprentice family workshop system, a youngster would start his training to be a *nishiki-e* blockcarver by cutting lettering. He then moved up to written characters of the prompt books used by the chanters in Kabuki or puppet theaters. From there he learned to remove the excess areas of the color woodblocks of *nishiki-e*. Finally he practiced cutting the outlines for less important parts like the costumes, hands and feet. After more practice only one of the most talented would come to carve facial outlines, until finally he could try the finest carving needed for the elaborate hair-styles of the finishing block. It took at least ten years of apprenticeship to learn the range of blockcarving techniques. Even with the present generation of master blockcarvers (who learned the craft just before or after the Second World War), most had to work until the age of forty or fifty before a select few were considered experienced enough to be entrusted with carving the fine details depicting the heads in prints of beautiful women.

"Carving the Woodblocks," from a composition of six prints, "Making Edo's Famous Souvenir the Full-color Print: Shown as a Parody of Rice Cultivation" (*Edo meibutsu nishiki-e kōsaku*), ca 1800. Kitagawa UTAMARO. Full-color, *ōban* print. Published by Tsuruya Kiemon. The British Museum.

Utamaro substitutes beautiful women (a common artistic practice) here for the male printmakers. The composition seems to have provided the inspiration for Kunisada's later print design (see p. 8). Both works present valuable information about early printmaking. Here, an assistant sharpens a straight-blade knife on a wet stone. At center, a blockcarver pauses before cutting the keyblock, and another carver clears areas of a block with chisel and mallet.

The Woodblocks

From the 19th century, or perhaps earlier, the blockcarver procured woodblocks from an artisan who specialized in seasoning and planing the boards for printer's woodblocks, rather than from the usual lumber dealer. *Ukiyo-e* blockcarvers preferred a variety of wild cherry wood. It was relatively available (much came from the Izu pennisula). The wood had a fine grain that was fairly easy to carve, yet hard enough to last through repeated printings. The more expensive and harder *tsuke* (boxwood) was used mainly for repair plugs. Woodblocks were routinely re-used by carving a different composition on the back or sometimes, especially for detail-less woodblocks for color impressions, by planing down a no longer needed carved surface. Use further seasoned the wood making it easier to carve; also, carvers preferred to work with old blocks because any imperfections in the grain which might adversely affect the carving would already have been revealed. The thickness of a typical woodblock which started at almost $1\frac{1}{4}$ inches (3.2cm) might end up less than half that before the block could no longer be used.

Carving the Keyblock from the Artist's Design

The carver's first step was the delicate job of affixing the artist's drawing to the block. He evenly spread rice-starch or wheat paste with his fingers and palm onto the surface of the board. Then he affixed the artist's master design, face down, smoothing out from the center. Only the most experienced craftsman could keep the thin paper from bubbling or distorting.

The blockcarver, usually after turning a vertical composition horizontal, stabilized the block at his low table, with his sharpened tools at ready on the side. He held the pointed straight-blade knife in his right hand resting between thumb and forefinger. Pushing the pommel down and forward (sometimes with his left hand) he followed around the artist's brushstrokes visible in the paper, cutting through the paper in order to carve the all-important keyblock (*omohan*). The paper sometimes was oiled with sesame-oil to increase its transparency. He cut away to leave ridges which, when inked, printed the black, even outlines of the design. He or his assistants used different size chisels with slightly rounded blades to clear empty areas of the composition, starting with small areas within figures, then moving on to the background. These chisels were struck with a mallet.

In a final step he carved the *kentō* guide marks. One was an L-shaped depression, usually at the bottom left corner, just outside the boundaries of the carved area of the composition. About two-thirds of the way along an adjoining side he cut a straight ridge (often referred to separately as the *hikitsuke*), in line with one of the legs of the "L". Today the carver uses a special square-headed chisel for the guide marks. Typically it could take a week of work to carve the keyblock.

The fact that a few artist's master designs are still extant suggests that, in order to prevent the master image from being destroyed in the carving, it was sometimes transferred to another sheet. This copy was then glued to the block.

A late 19th-century record says that in earlier periods the carver at first cut the outlines for the

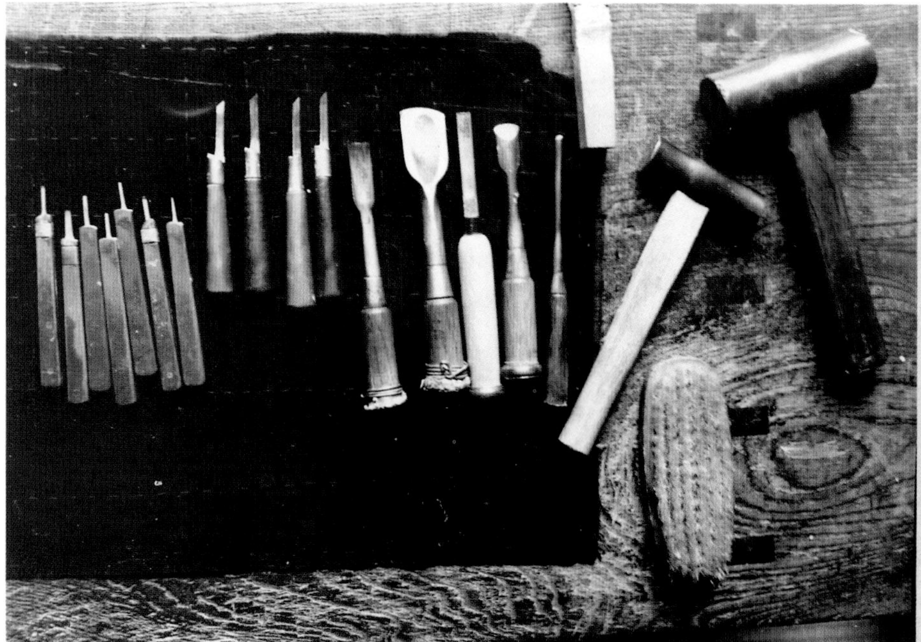

The Modern Blockcarver's Tools.
(From left) gougers (mostly for corrections), straight-blade knives (sharpened to a point), various chisels, weight, mallets for hitting chisels, and brush for cleaning block.

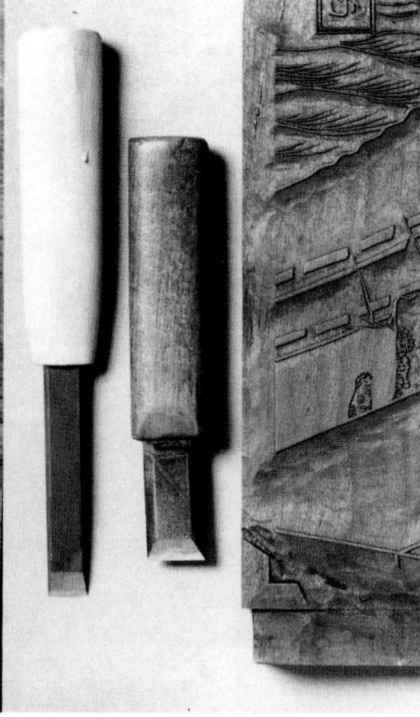

Square-headed chisels for making the *kentō* guide marks.

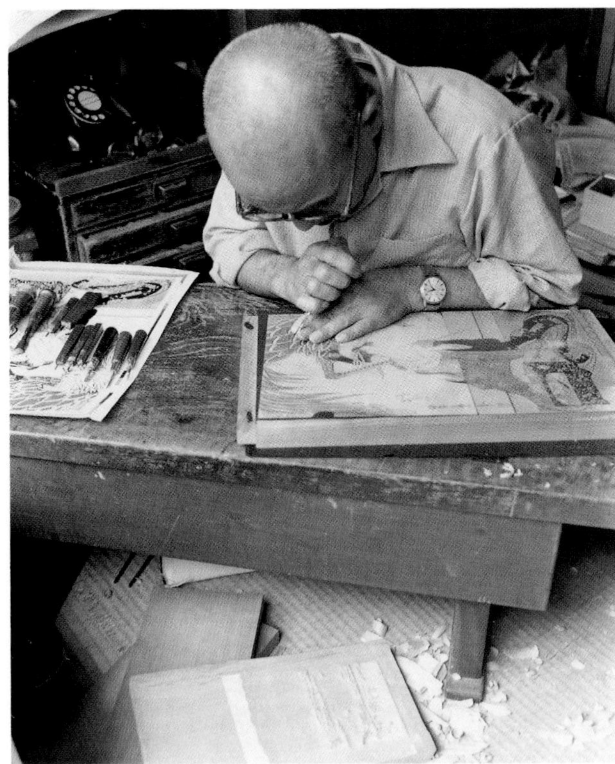
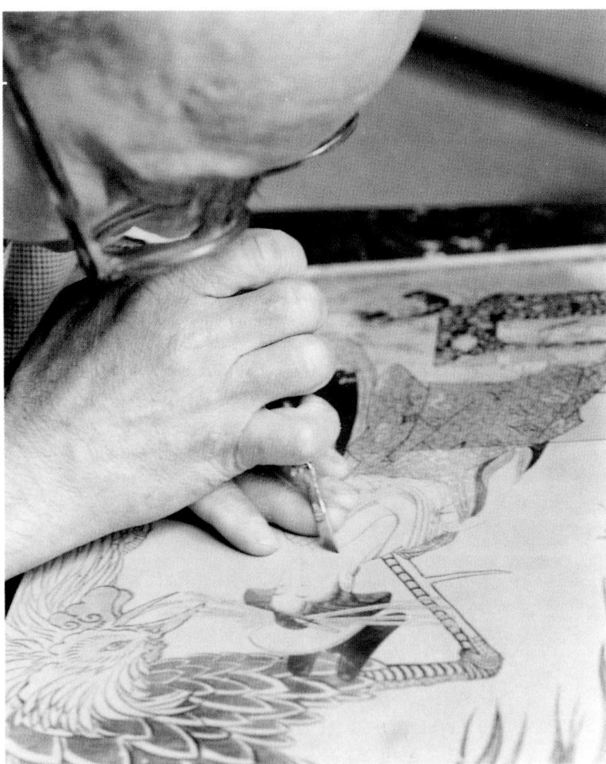

Blockcarver, Itoh Susumu, carves the keyblock outlines with a straight-blade pointed knife, cutting through a photograph tracing (substituting for the artist's drawing) pasted on the block, in the process of carving blocks for a modern reproduction.

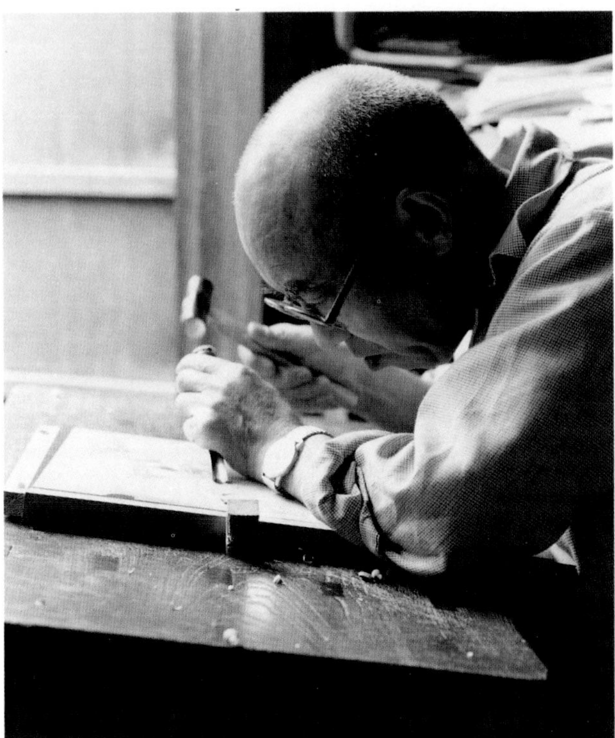

Clearing areas not to be printed using a chisel and mallet.

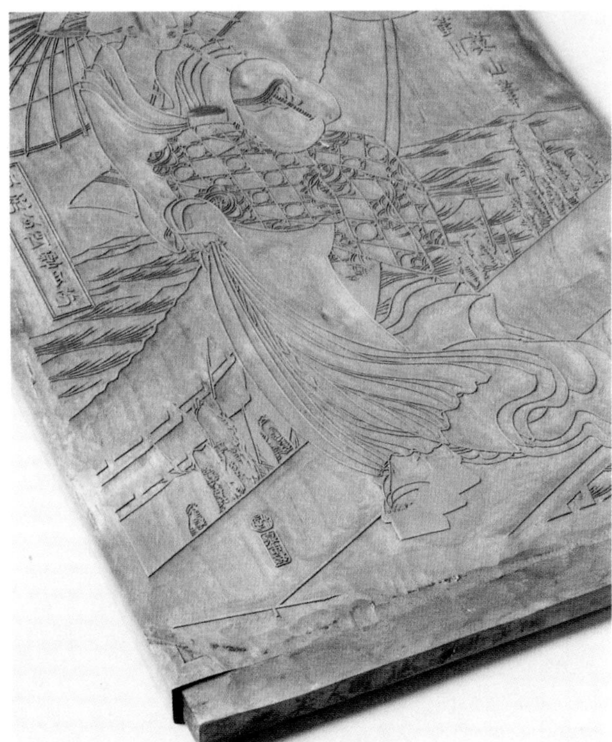

Keyblock for the modern reproduction of "Snow." Wood slat attached (at bottom) to prevent warping and ease handling.

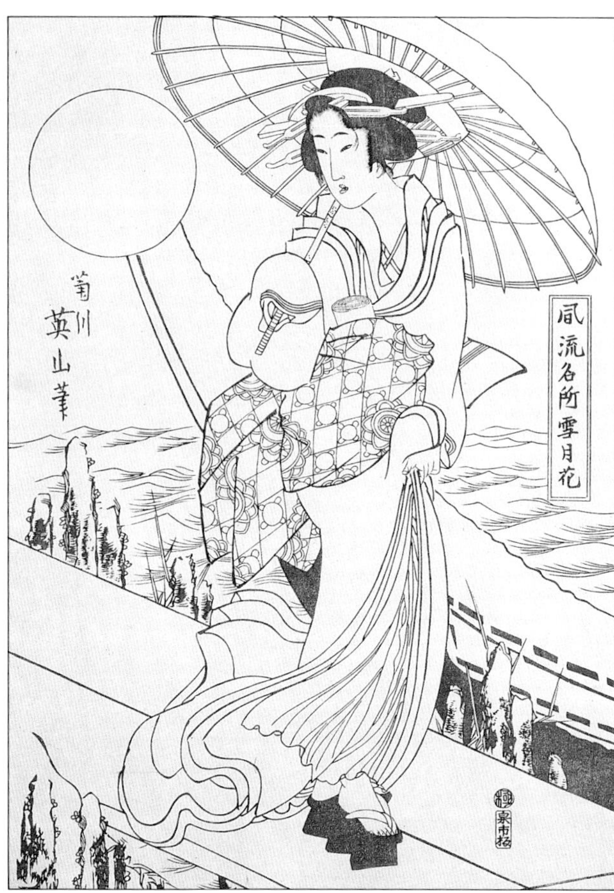

A keyblock proof of the Eizan print "Snow," with all the outlines of the composition printed in black *sumi.*

keyblock wider than were needed, with deep cuts, and then later narrowed the ridges in a second carving step. By the middle decades of the 19th century the overall carving of keyblocks had become shallower. The engraver saved time by carving the outline ridges to their required narrowness from the outset. This called for more precise, and so shallower, cuts. From the late nineteenth century, chisels with u-shaped blades, and later, v-shaped blades, came into use which further speeded the clearing away of areas between lines of the composition.

Some extant keyblocks for late period actor and *sumo* wrestler prints have replaceable inlay plugs for faces and name cartouches, since demand for a certain face or name lasted only briefly. The rest of the keyblock (with the carving of the figure below the neck) was used again and again for different prints. On a finished print two thin-line breaks in the outline of a figure's neck at the collar are evidence of a plugged keyblock (and so a later edition). Also in the 19th century, as print quality declined, responsibility for the keyblocks of some multiprint compositions was given to different carvers to speed up the carving process.

The carver, after brushing off and thoroughly moistening the keyblock, then charged it with black (*sumi*) and printed a few initial trial prints. Thus he had to have many of the printer's tools in his workshop. To lessen chances of distortion he printed on more expensive *mino* paper. These trial proofs showing all the important outlines of the composition, without any fine details, would go back to the artist for him to check. The artist often indicated colors for the final printing by writing a color term ("blue," "pink," etc.) on an individual proof and indicating the areas for that color with red.

Correcting the Woodblock

When the blockcarver made small mistakes during the initial cutting he would correct the woodblock in the same way the artist's minor changes on the keyblock proof were incorporated into the keyblock. The blockcarver gouged out the offending ridge or small area which had been carved too far and then tapped in an inlay of a whittled-down wood-pin. Cut down to the original level of the block the plugged area could then be recarved. A bad slip during carving or a significant proof correction could not be corrected. Veteran carver Itoh Susumu relates that in the course of his career spanning more than fifty years only on one or two "really bad days" has he had to start a block over.

After the artist returned the annotated keyblock proofs to the blockcarver he usually had no further involvement in the print-making process. This fact reflects the importance of the keyblock in transmitting the artistic intentions of the designer. On the other hand, it also indicates the large input made by the carver and then the printer on the finished product.

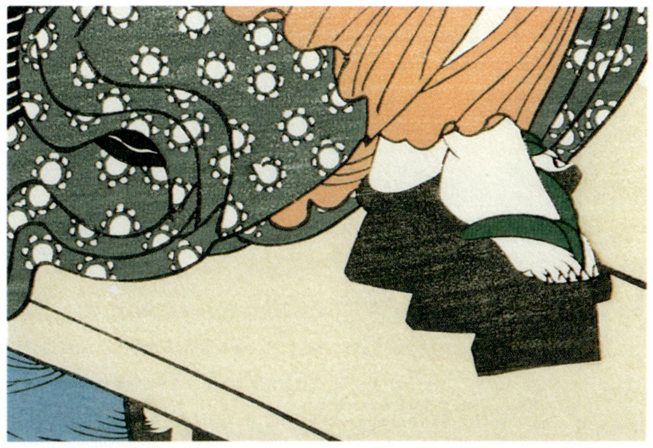

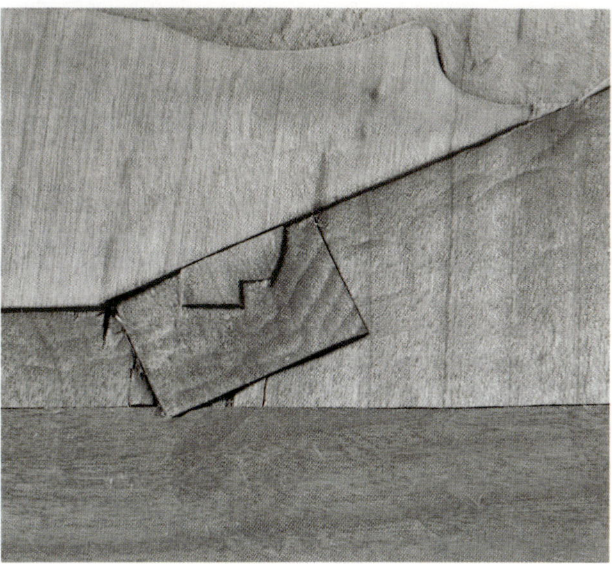

Typical Correction of a Woodblock. (above) The small area rendering a piling under the dock and geisha's feet (in the print "Snow"). The carver overlooked the piling during the initial carving of the block for pale red (p. 52), and so a plug was inserted and the area re-carved. The plugged correction can be seen in the woodblock (below). No trace of the plug, which was cut to follow the design (as was usually the case), is visible on the print.

Carving the Rest of the Woodblock Set

Each subsequent woodblock for each color (which might consist of only tiny areas in the middle of the sheet) was carved following a pasted on keyblock print with color indications (usually by the artist) and included the same *kentō* guides cut for the keyblock. A typical full-color print required about ten woodblocks, with prints requiring a set of twenty blocks not uncommon.

Not every colored area on a finished print called for its own block, because overprinting two colors could be used to produce a third color. Sometimes the carver, to save on expense and the difficulty of handling so many blocks, cut different areas of the same woodblock for different color impressions to be made at separate times. The printer was able to use different places on the same block, realigning the sheets of paper with a different *kentō* each run, either because the block-carver carved different *kentō* for each impression or else because the printer himself would recut the *kentō* for each color.

The carvers cut extra blocks as needed for special effects: mica backgrounds, gauffrage, burnishing (an unusual procedure which required the block be carved as the finished print, not as its reverse image), or gold and silver details on *surimono*. Moreover, the carver needed to cut at least two blocks besides the keyblock just for black. Often included was a block for pale-black that served to intensify the effect of black lines (especially in the hairstyles) by hiding the white paper. Then there was the finishing woodblock for black details.

A viewer's response to a print is often created by the artistry of these details (for example the fine lines of hair along a woman's hairline) produced by the finishing block. Extant artist's master drawings abbreviate such details, leaving the responsibility for them up to the skill and judgement of the master blockcarver. Something of what we consider an artist's "style" may be in fact the characteristic carving of details by his master carver.

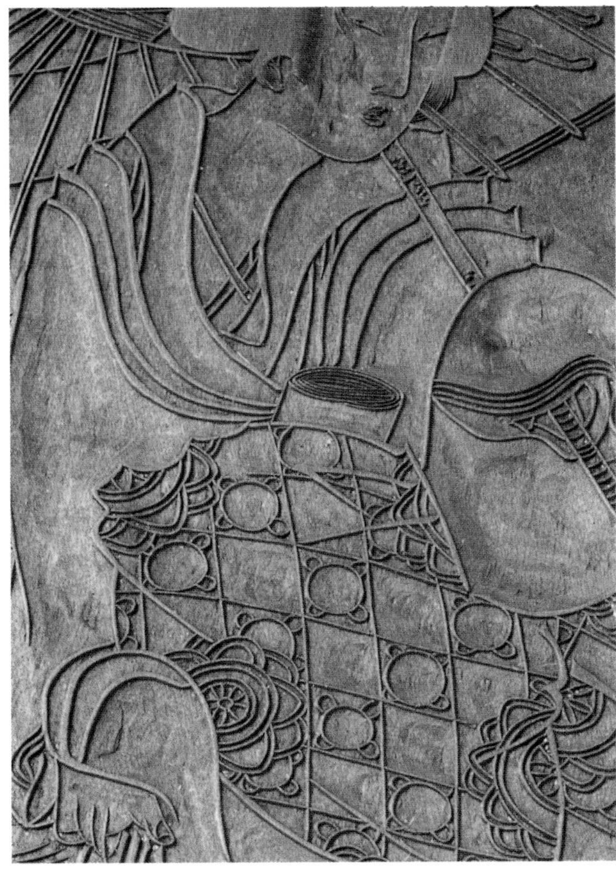

Detail of the keyblock showing the cleared areas and even, narrow ridges which produce the black outlines.

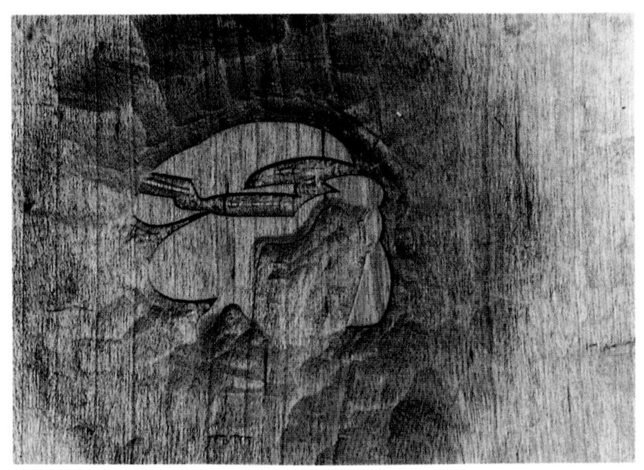

Detail of a Typical "Black-intensifier" Woodblock. This woodblock produces a solid area of grey-black that, by hiding the white of the paper, intensifies the effect of the black lines (printed later) which depict the elaborate hair-style.

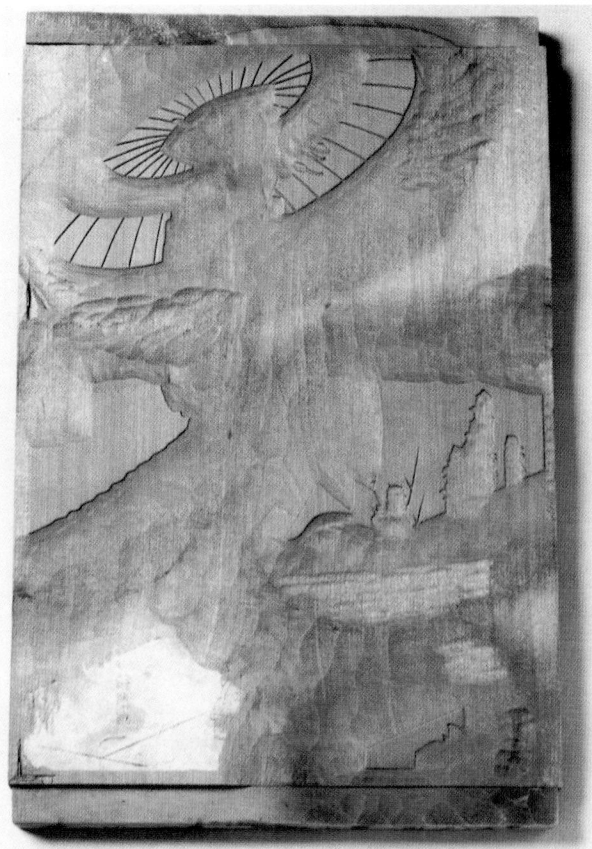

The same woodblock carved to use both for red and deep blue color impressions (made at separate times) when printing the reproduction of the Eizan print "Snow."

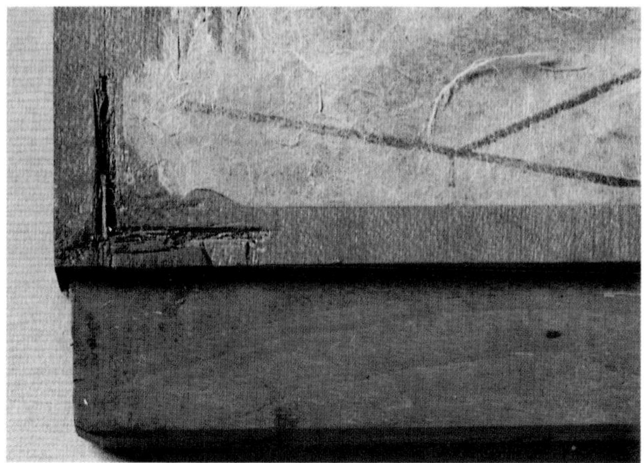

Close up of a woodblock for a colored area where the *kentō* was re-gouged. Realignment was needed to keep the impressions in register.

The Printer

Almost as strict training as for the blockcarver was required of the printer. Some evidence that *ukiyo-e* printing had become an independent responsibility and guild, separate from both block-carving and from printing book-texts, exists from around 1763 when color printing was fast developing. The fact that the name of the printer appears on a print even less frequently than the rare appearence of the blockcarver's (even after the end of the Edo period) suggests that the publisher contracted the printing out at the last moment, once the woodblocks had been carved. The printer's status in the 18th and 19th centuries was lower than that of a master carver. The saying goes that, no matter how skillful the printer, he could not last much beyond his fortieth year. Strength and stamina were important. The printer with a few tools could work almost anywhere, but by the 19th century the printer of *ukiyo-e* seems to have been based in a home-work-shop located in the neighborhood of the publisher and blockcarver.

Full-color Trial Proofs and Final Correction of the Woodblocks

The printer, after having received the carved woodblocks and general instructions about coloring, first made several full-color trial prints. These allowed the printer to adjust the color harmonies to his satisfaction. The printer seems to have had a great deal of independence in choosing the hue and intensity of colors. Sometimes through discussion with the publisher (virtually never with the artist), he made last minute corrections to the composition. He also checked that small colored areas were not inadvertently missing or that colors were not misaligned. The printer recut the *kentō* or made the corrections in the woodblocks himself, rather than sending the

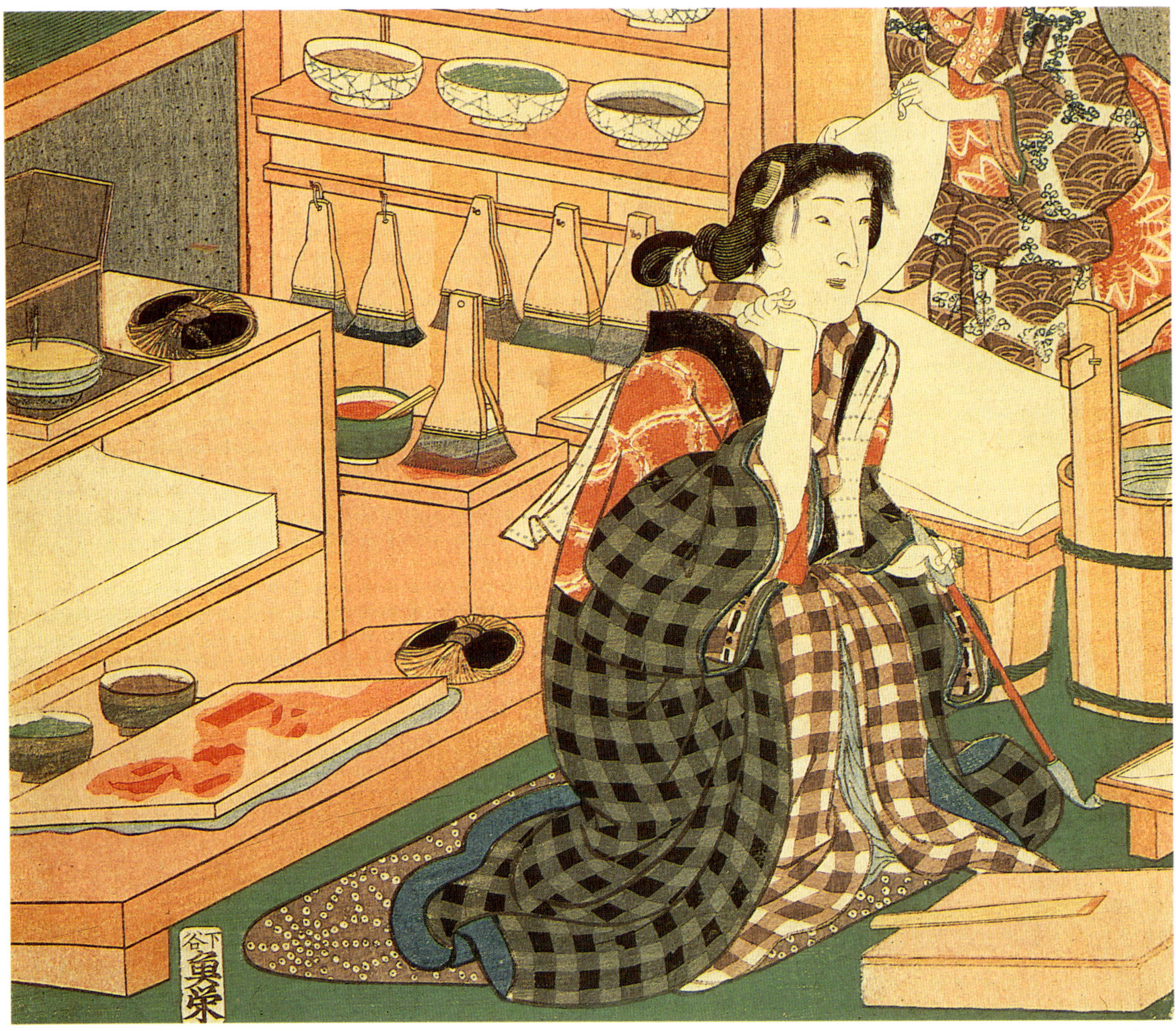

Detail showing a beauty as the printer taking a smoking break at "his" work-area. From Kunisada's "Parody of Samurai, Farmers, Artisans, and Merchants in the Latest Fashions: Artisans." 1857. Private collection. See text discussion pp. 38 and 41. Title page shows entire scene.

blocks back to the carver's atelier. In addition to the carver's straight-blade knife and chisels, the printer came to count among his tools the gouger and small saw for making plug corrections. He used the same techniques of gouging out the offending line or area and inlaying a plug.

During the course of handling and printing, the moisture content of the blocks and the paper changed particularly when there were changes in the weather. This was one reason why most printing was done in the winter months when humidity levels were low and relatively stable.

Even with precautions and working quickly, the printer, often in mid run, had to adjust for the subtle expansion or shrinkage of the woodblocks, and had to moisten or "rest" a block, or re-carve a *kentō*.

Today, the modern printer usually maintains close communication with the blockcarver and relies on him to make any corrections or changes in the woodblocks. Alignment of colors remains the printer's responsibility, however, and so every printer still owns a *kentō* chisel and makes the frequent carving adjustments to the guide marks.

The Pigments

The printer, whether for trial proofs or the full-edition, first had to ready the black (*sumi*) and the water-based organic and inorganic or mineral color pigments. *Sumi* from early times was available commercially. By the 19th century the printer could buy most other pigments in semi-processed form. Still, it took time and patient mixing to achieve the right consistency. To make black, for example, he took a prepared bar of soot which had been produced by burning charcoal or oil and molded into bars by adding glue and aromatics. He dissolved the bar in water either in one of his small bowls for pigments or on an ink-stone, aided with a spatula (see Utamaro print, p. 43). Then he strained the liquid through fine cloth; a step that was usually unnecessary when preparing *sumi* for writing or painting with a brush. To get a glossy black (used for example in depictions of hair) he added an appropriate amount of *nikawa* (animal collagen glue). The colors were mixed in small bowls with a pestle to remove any lumps.

Problems remain in deciding what pigments originally were used on old *nishiki-e*. Many of the colors have faded or chemically changed. Japanese researchers are loath to sample fragile originals and Edo-period written records about pigments are scarce. The consensus at present, which is based mainly on research in western conservation labs, holds that the pigments which might have been used on a typical full-color print from the late 18th or early 19th century were as follows. Blues came from indigo (*ai*) or day-flower (*tsuyugusa*). The printer rather than using the indigo plant directly started with a bar pigment made from leeching the blue from old fabrics. He eventually could buy the *tsuyugusa* light-blue (originally from flower petals) as strips of dyed paper (*ai-gami*) which he soaked in water to produce his pigment. *Tsuyugusa* blue was extremely fugitive, even more so than indigo, and rarely has survived on old prints. Rose-red (*beni*) came from safflowers, and was another light-sensitive colorant.

Organic yellows, which also tended to fade easily, came from tropical tumeric root (*ukon*) or gamboge (*kusashio*) from a tree sap (*sp. Gracinia*). While other yellows, called *enju*, *kihada*, and a mustard green called *zumi* came from flowers and plant barks. Rather than printing a white, most often the printer utilized the paper itself for white areas. Some sources suggest organic white (*gofun*) from powdered oyster shell was sometimes used. Chemical analysis has discovered inorganic white lead carbonate (*empaku*) on a few prints. *Empaku* blackens over time, a condition today misleadingly known as *gofun-yaki*.

The inorganic pigments did tend to be more colorfast. Among them, orange-red (*tan*) made from lead, sulphur and saltpeter, however, also tended to blacken over time. Vermilion (*shu*) was mercuric sulfide. Other reds (*benigara*) were ferric oxide pigments made from heating hematite (naturally occuring in earth) or ferrous sulphate. A bright yellow (*shio*), was a highly toxic naturally occuring compound of sulfer and arsenic. Other traditional mineral paints, such as malachite for green, proved too coarse-grained to print successfully.

Combinations of the above pigments, each mixed in a small bowl before printing, seem to have produced the other pigment colors available to the 18th or early 19th century printer: gamboge and *tsuyugusa* blue or *zumi* yellow and indigo gave the greens. Gamboge and safflower rose or *benigara* and black *sumi*, produced orange-browns. Gamboge and *shu* produced a light-brown (*chōji*).

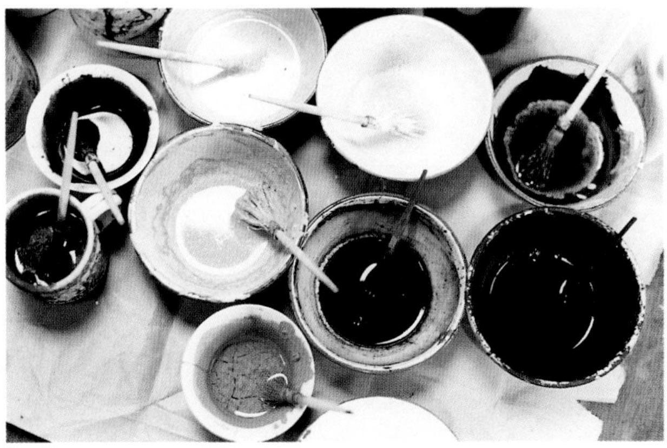

Pigments readied in small bowls with flicker brushes.

Zumi yellow and safflower rose or *benigara* gave an orange pigment (*dai'ō*). Lavender, a mixture of safflower rose and *tsuyugusa* blue, was extremely sensitive to light and moisture.

Rarely colorants might be mixed on the woodblock itself—for example a little yellow added to a red to give it zest. Overlaying colors in two or more impressions during separate printings gave intermediate colors. In general, however, the *nishiki-e* printer avoided muted tones or greyish hues; the Edo public preferred straight, bright colors.

In the 1790's mica came to be used to produce glistening irridescent backgrounds, such as in Utamaro or Sharaku prints, and for small details especially on *surimono*. From around the same decade printers also employed for *surimono* metallic powder pigments, sometimes cheaper look alikes, more often the real silver or gold. Most accounts say that around 1820, but perhaps before, Prussian blue, called *berorinai* (an artificial pigment first made in Europe in 1704) was imported from Holland. It provided the strong blue used in the skies of many Hokusai and Hiroshige prints.

Aniline dyes, which produce the unrelenting reds, purples and other colors of Meiji period prints (see example, p. 6), came into fashion after the middle of the nineteenth century, and had mostly replaced traditional pigments by the 1870's.

Preparing the Paper

Another step, before the actual printing, was to cut and then to size the paper. The printer, or assistants, evenly applied a sizing (*nikawa* and alum thinned in warm water) to the paper with a large broad brush. They then hung the sheets on a line to dry as we see in the Utamaro print. Without this size the colors would run during printing or seep through to the next sheet in the pile. The sizing also prevented any soft, shorter fibers of the paper from adhering to the block or from pilling. The lower the paper quality, the more sizing needed; the more sizing used, however, the darker the yellow cast given to the paper.

The printer kept the sized sheets slightly damp by interspersing a wet sheet with every three or four sheets in the pile of paper ready to be printed for an edition. The pile was kept in a draft-free place (within a shelf: Kunisada print, p. 36) and sometimes was wrapped in a cloth. Preserving the correct moisture content was vital in printing consistent colors. However, if the paper were too moist the colors could bleed, or if the workshop were too warm and humid the paper molded during the days it took to print an edition.

"Applying the Size," subtitled "Flooding the Paddy for Transplanting," one print from Utamaro's "Making Edo's Famous Souvenir the Full-color Print: Shown as a Parody of Rice Cultivation," ca 1800. Full-color, *ōban* print. The British Museum.
The printer and assistants apply dilute sizing from a bucket with a broad brush and hang the sheets up to dry.

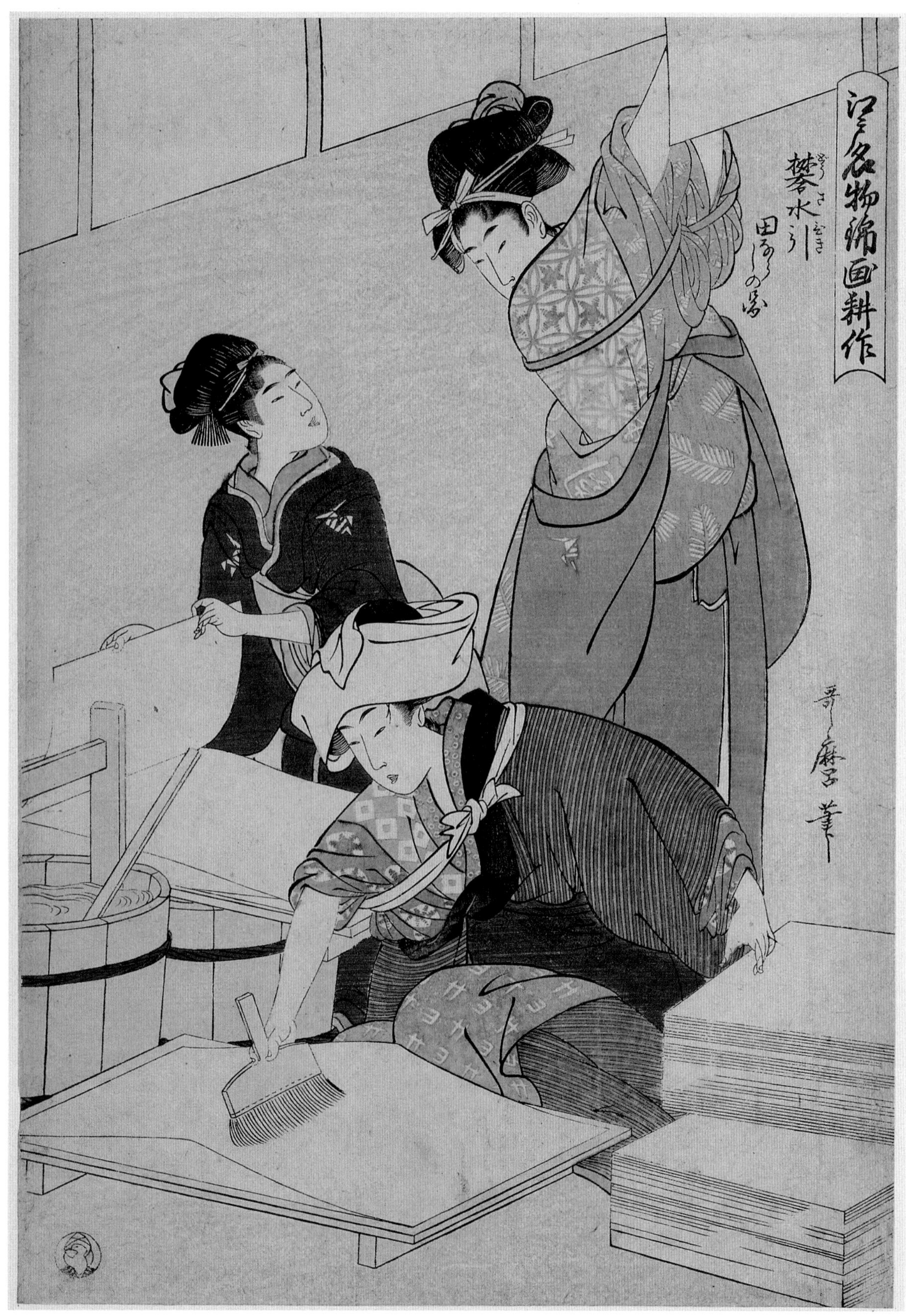
江戸名物錦画耕作
さらき
摂水引
田□□の男
歌麿筆

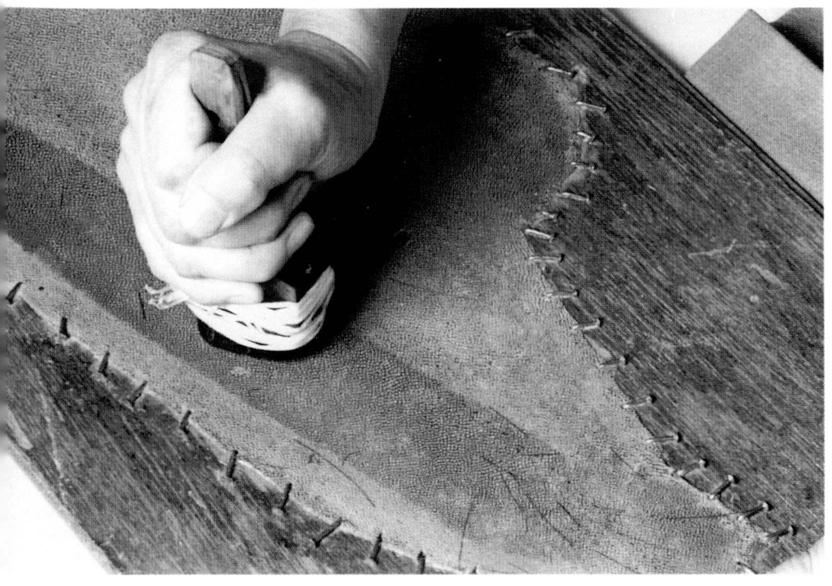

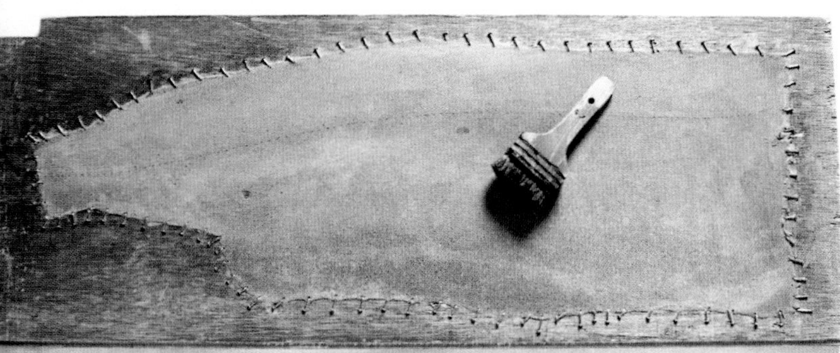

Softening and Evening the Bristles of a Typical Old-style Brush. The bristles (usually horse-hair) were often scorched and then tied with string to stabilize during the brisk rubbing along a stretched shark skin.

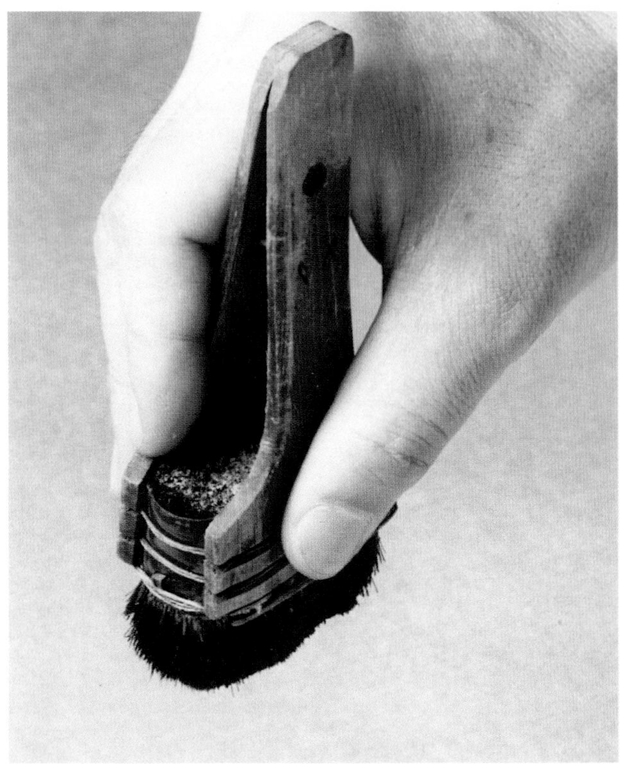

Medium size handled-brush, typically used for spreading pigment on the woodblock.

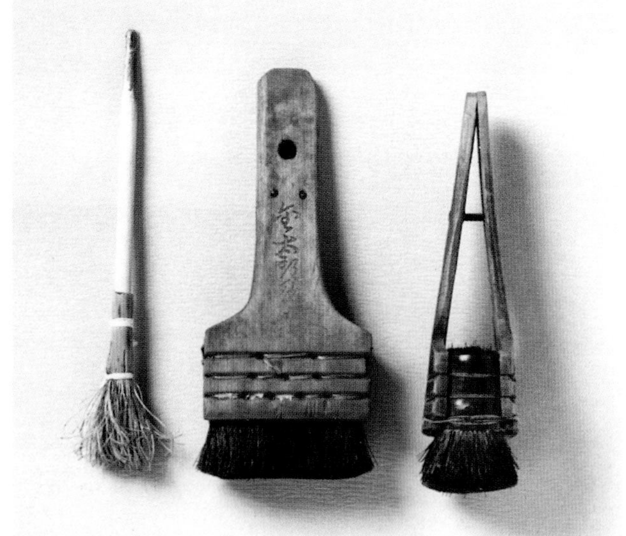

Small flicker brush (of slit bamboo leaves) next to two small handled-brushes (one in profile to show how bristles fit between split handle).

Readying the Block and Applying Pigment

Both Utamaro's and Kunisada's prints depicting the printing process show that from the early 19th century (if not before) the printer anchored the woodblock to be printed on his low table with cloth, and tilted it slightly away from himself. Printers today use small pads of cloth at the corners, often together with a dampened cloth folded to the size of the block. The printer usually worked seated behind a shelf or small screen in order to keep drafts and dust away from his work. Kunisada's print (detail, p. 36) shows a small burning stick of incense on the shelf, perhaps to indicate unsuspected drafts. The printer kept his work area neat and his habits orderly, for example using a different brush for each pigment. His many brushes and pigments in small bowls are neatly and prominently arranged in the Kunisada print. The printer bought his wide handled-brushes from a shop or dealer. He softened the animal-hair bristles of his handled-brushes when new or, periodically, as they wore down through use, by rubbing them along a stretched shark skin. Since the late 19th century, the traditional handled-brushes for spreading the pigments on the woodblock have been largely replaced by flat, rectangular brushes with rounded corners, which fit into the palm.

Ready for the actual printing, he moistened the block face. Then with a small flicker brush, made of bamboo leaves, he daubed on the black or chosen pigment. He added and mixed rice-starch paste with the pigment on the block itself, using a handled-brush to achieve the right consistency. Tapping and rotating the entire brush, as well as using the broad strokes you might expect, he evenly saturated the raised areas of the block, not worrying about getting the color in the carved out areas.

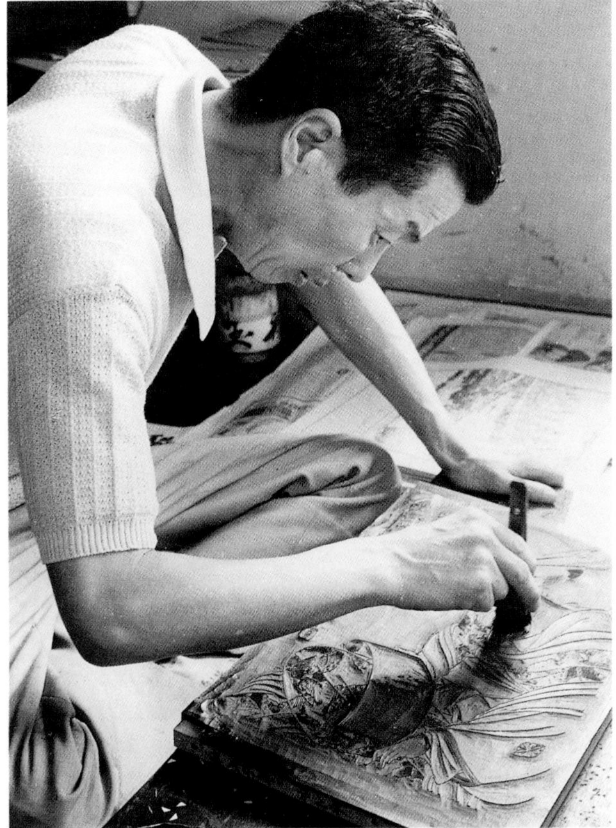

Modern printer Kajikawa Yoshio, seated cross-legged at the traditional low table, applies black *sumi* to a keyblock.

For most *nishiki-e* he spread the color pigment evenly on the block. For special effects such as for the depiction of sky on 19th-century prints or for motifs on *surimono* he modulated the application. By adding a little extra water with a rag (wrapped around a small block of wood or stone) to the woodblock before applying pigment he could achieve a band of darker or lighter hue at the top of a printed sky or otherwise introduce a kind of shading (*bokashi*) within an area of color. The printer never added white or black to modulate a colored area. When later 19th-century print artists (moving away from the strict *ukiyo-e* style) called for black or grey shading to indicate volume or shadows this shading, of course, required a separate block and impression.

Printing

The printer took up a sheet of paper from his pile and placed it face down on the woodblock. He fit a corner of the sheet into the L-shaped *kentō* depression and alligned the paper edge with the straight groove along the one side to ensure register.

He printed with no mechanical press by rubbing firmly from the back with a *baren*, the circular disk of batting covered with bamboo-leaf sheeting twisted to form a grip. How firmly? It's said with strong enough pressure to work up a sweat on a winter's day. To help prevent the paper from slipping the printer usually started from a lower corner near the *kentō* and moved the *baren*, as he rubbed along, in a semi-circular direction ending in an upper corner. Sometimes, marks of the *baren* or of a faint woodgrain from the block remain visible on a finished print and give interest to broad areas of color. He pulled off the sheet and placed it in a finished pile to await the next color impression once all the sheets had been printed off the first block.

Occasionally the block was immediately re-inked and the same sheet printed again to intensify a color. This was routine for colored backgrounds when often the printer lifted only half the sheet and re-inked only a part of the block to print again. Backgrounds required several such repetitions.

The printer recharged the block with color pigment for each sheet. Periodically he oiled the *baren* with sesame-oil until it wore out. The printer was skilled at making his own *baren*. Utamaro's print (r.) catches the printer at the moment of twisting one together. "He" seems to be too busy to have put away the woodblock he was printing from, which is seen underneath the board used as a work surface to make the new *baren*.

As a rule, consistent color on all the prints in an edition was difficult to achieve without a lot of wasted trial impressions unless the same person printed a given color off the woodblock without lengthly interruptions. Depending on the complexity of the carving and the pigment which was

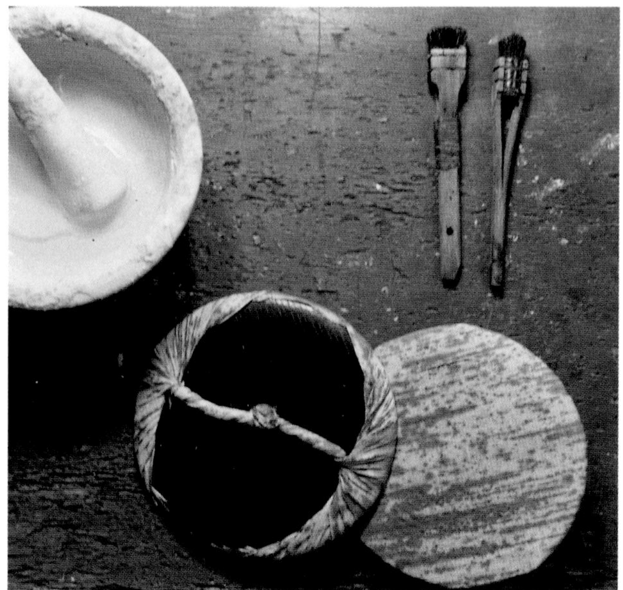

Close-up of two *baren*.

"The Printers," subtitled "Transplanting the Rice Seedlings," from Utamaro's "Making Edo's Famous Souvenir the Full-color Print: Shown as a Parody of Rice Cultivation," ca 1800. Full-color, *ōban* print. The British Museum.

The printer at left is using the *baren* to print. The printer at right is depicted making a new *baren* (scissors and bamboo strips at "his" right). Besides small bowls with pigments there are two large inkstones for preparing the black *sumi*. It appears some sort of spatula was used for the *sumi*. At right a pile of paper sits (weighted by a board) ready for printing.

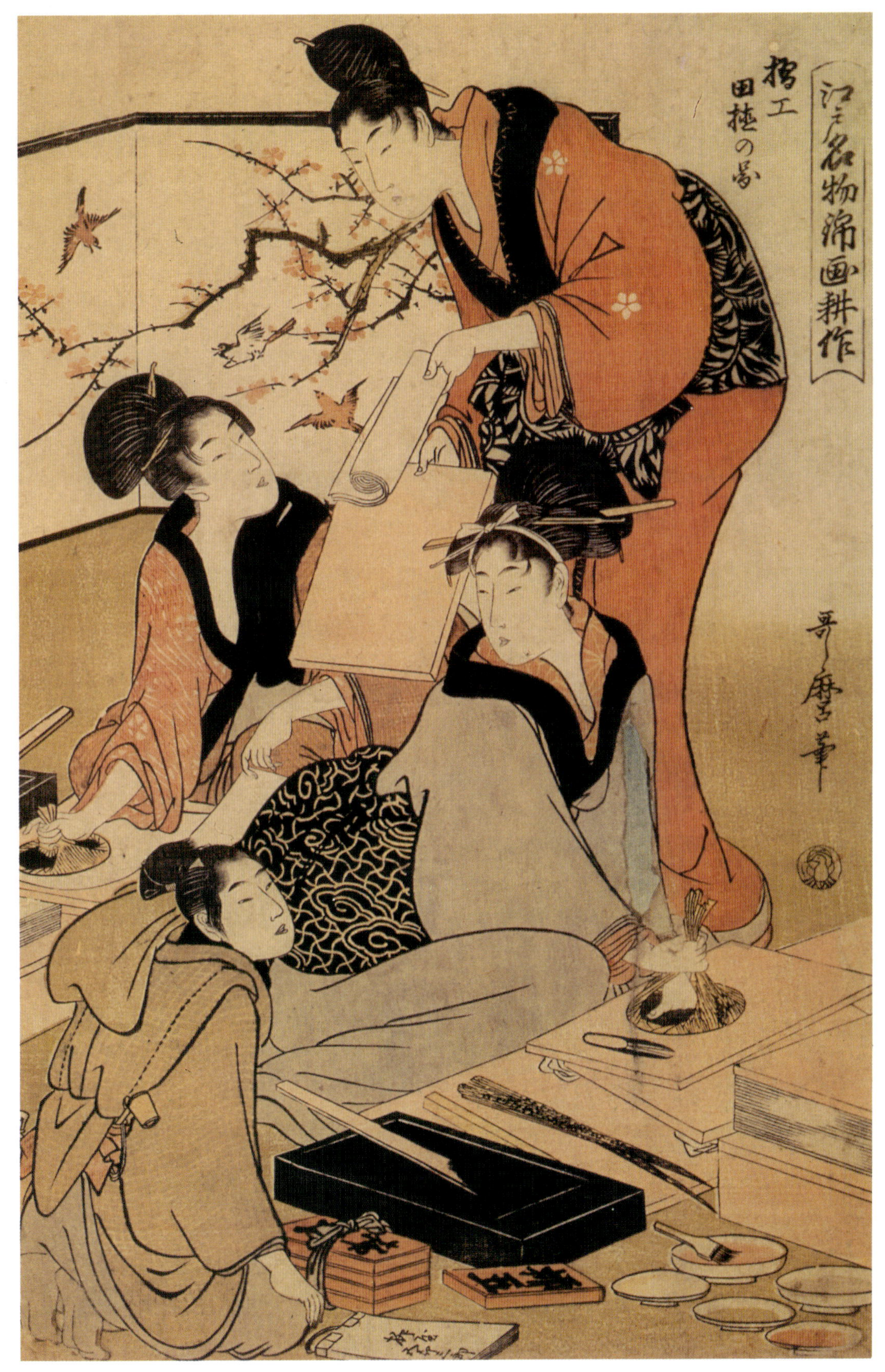

江戸名物錦画耕作
搗工
田埴の図
哥麿筆

used, a printer typically could make up to two hundred impressions off one block without an extended, such as overnight, work break.

Written records after the 1860's frequently mention a printer's unit of work, *ippai*, which is taken to mean 200 impressions. This number was not only around the limit of a man's energy per workday, but a woodblock tended to become over-saturated with pigment at around 200 impressions and no longer printed crisply. Indeed, the paler colors such as the organic yellows quickly oversaturated the block well before 200 impressions could be made. The notion that a woodblock "wears down" after 200 impressions seems to be a common misapprehension. Contemporary printers can take many more than 200 impressions off a block. Detail-less woodblocks for colored areas withstood much more use and pressure (which was routinely applied) than the keyblock or the finishing block for fine details. But even in the case of a woodblock with extensive fine-line detail, it could print hundreds of impressions without noticeable wear.

Written documentation is scarce, but 200 may also have been the number of finished prints in a typical late 18th-century edition. In the 1820's and 1830's when popular prints began to come out in documented editions of several thousand, the practice was to lightly clean and "rest" a saturated woodblock for several days after a run of about 200 impressions.

Unusual effects required extra blocks and time-consuming printing techniques. The most common method for mica backgrounds employed two identical blocks. The artisan printed an under-color (typically black *sumi* for grey, safflower rose for pink, a yellow; with no undercolor the mica alone printed a silver-white ground). Then coating another identically carved block with *nikawa* glue or rice-starch paste he printed to moisten the same background area and then sprinkled on fine mica flakes, and, finally, shook off the excess. Another method required the mica, pre-mixed with color and thinned glue, be printed in one step; another for the image to be blocked out with a stencil and the mica in sizing applied by brush.

Printing gold or silver (seen on *surimono* not commonly on *nishiki-e*) involved similar tech-

niques and an extra burnishing step. In one method the printer utilized one block for *nikawa* glue or paste and then sprinkled on the powdered metallic pigment. He then placed the thoroughly dried sheet backside down on another woodblock (carved exactly like the finished print rather than in reverse) so that the metallic area could be burnished directly, using a small block, traditionally a boar's tooth. On *nishiki-e*, direct burnishing from the front occurred for black or colored areas to produce such effects as the subtle black on black patterns of fabric motifs depicted on kimono.

In gauffrage or blind printing (*karazuri* and *kimedashi*) the printer made a separate impression with an un-inked woodblock to emboss parts of the design. The printing technique which usually called for a separate, deeply carved block and well dampened *hōsho* paper was basically the same as for an inked impression. The valleys or low areas in the carved woodblock made the gauffrage lines or relief that indicated snow, animal fur, or fabrics on, for example, the early *nishiki-e* of Harunobu and Bunchō. We find embossing most often on uncolored or only lightly colored areas of *nishiki-e*. Master printers achieved particularly beautiful texturing of gauffrage on *surimono*.

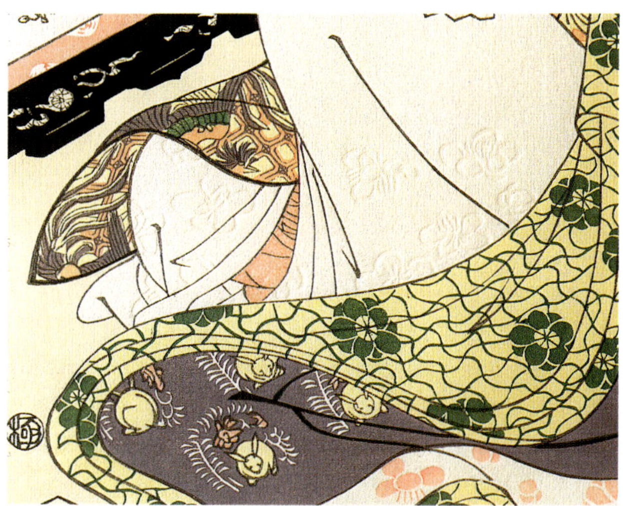

Detail of a modern reproduction of an Eishi woodblock print showing gauffrage (or embossed printing) in the depiction of the white kimono.

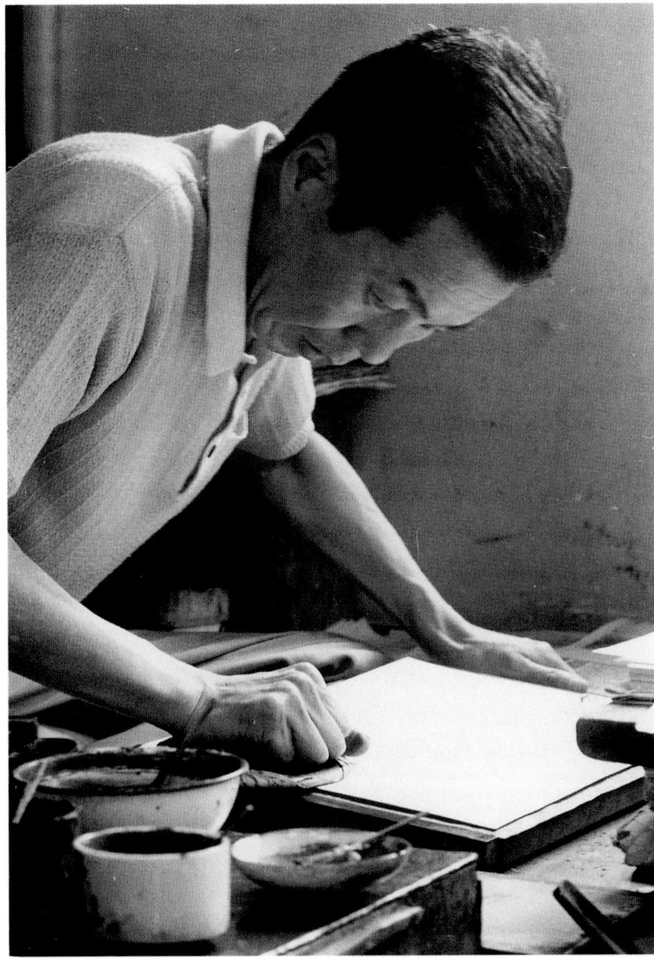

Printer Kajikawa Yoshio tenses with effort as he rubs the back of a sheet with the *baren* to take an impression.

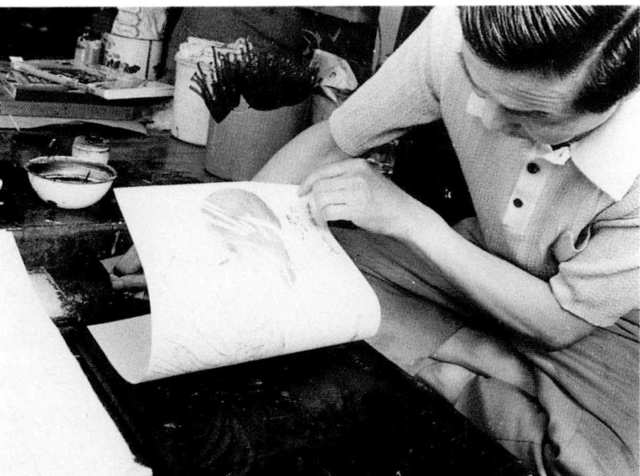

He peels off a printed sheet from the woodblock and checks the impression.

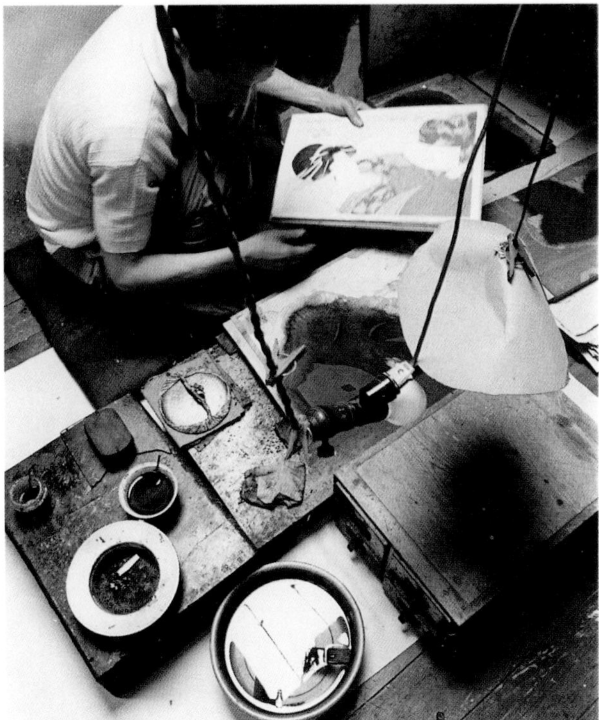

The modern printer's work area. Note the bowl of water in front for wetting the woodblock faces, thining pigments, or adding more moisture to the block to produce shading (*bokashi*). The modern flat brush for spreading pigments, which has largely replaced the old-style handled brushes, rests next to the *baren* (on an oiled cloth) at his right.

The Printing Order of Woodblocks for an Edition

A minimum of about 10 impressions were needed to print a representative *nishiki-e*. The printer took impressions off the various woodblocks in a standard, fixed order that Kajikawa Yoshio followed to print the modern reproduction of the Eizan print, "Snow". First the keyblock. Then woodblocks for paler colors or small areas of color (i.e. red for lips). Then followed woodblocks for strong colors. Most backgrounds, which were spare of details, in other words broad expanses of a single or solid color, were printed with repeated inkings toward the end. Last came the impressions off blocks intensifying black details and off the important finishing block(s) with its fine-line black details. The special effects of gauffrage or burnishing from the front would be destroyed with pressure or rubbing and so were naturally performed last. A typical *nishiki-e* edition could easily require two weeks to print.

Each impression used to produce a modern reproduction of the Eizan print "Snow" is shown separately on the following pages. The reproduction faithfully copies the extant Edo-period print down to the "mistake" of missing waves to the right of the title cartouche. And, although the number of woodblocks may be one or two more than for the first (ca 1810) edition, the order of taking impressions from the blocks in all likelihood nearly duplicates the original printing. The craftsman, it is well to remember, printed from a given block all the sheets in an edition, or at least a substantial pile, before he started to print from another woodblock in the set.

First, the keyblock impression (or proof) that produces the all important black outlines and includes the artist's signature, the title cartouche, censor's seal and publisher's mark.

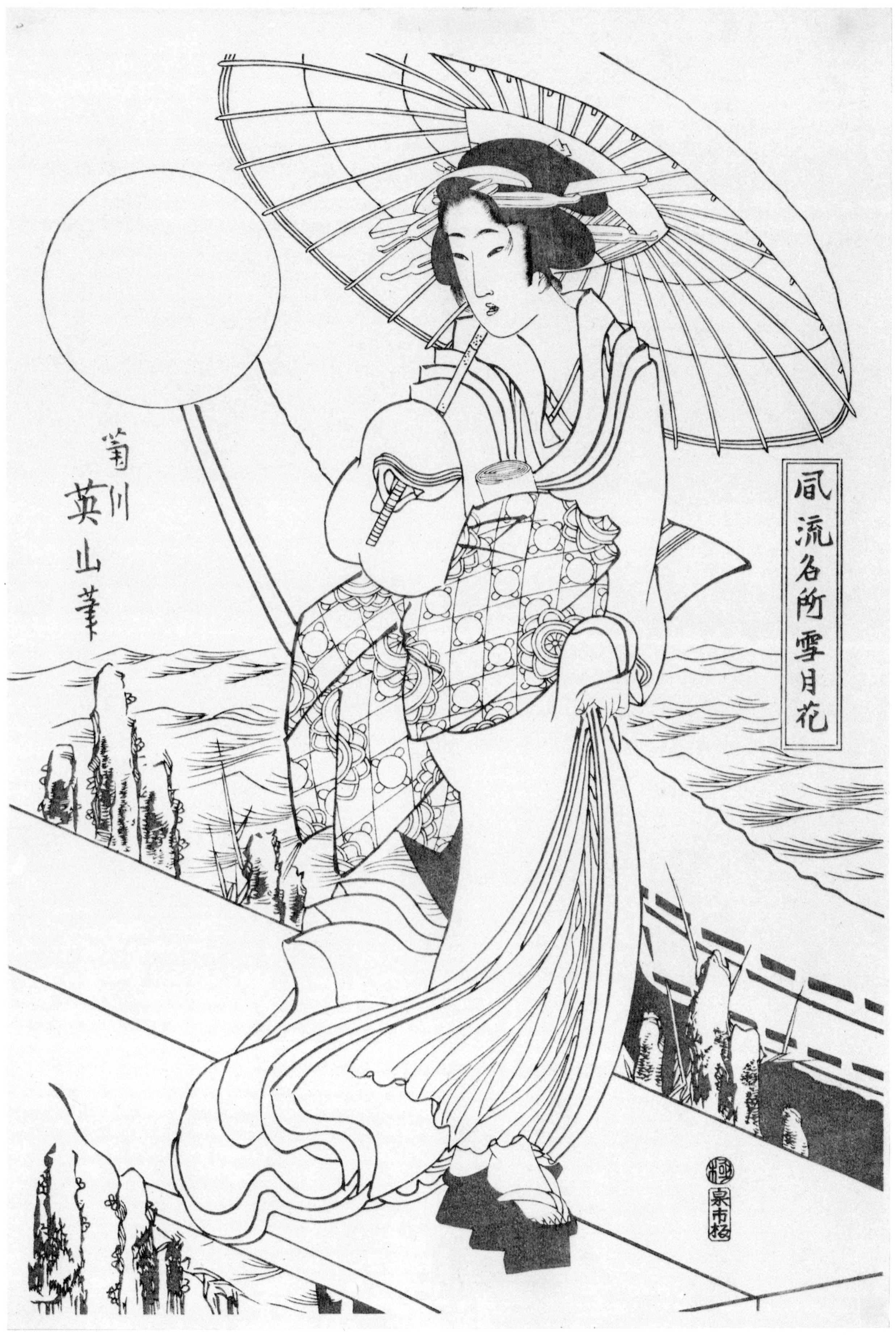
菊川
英山筆
風流名所雪月花

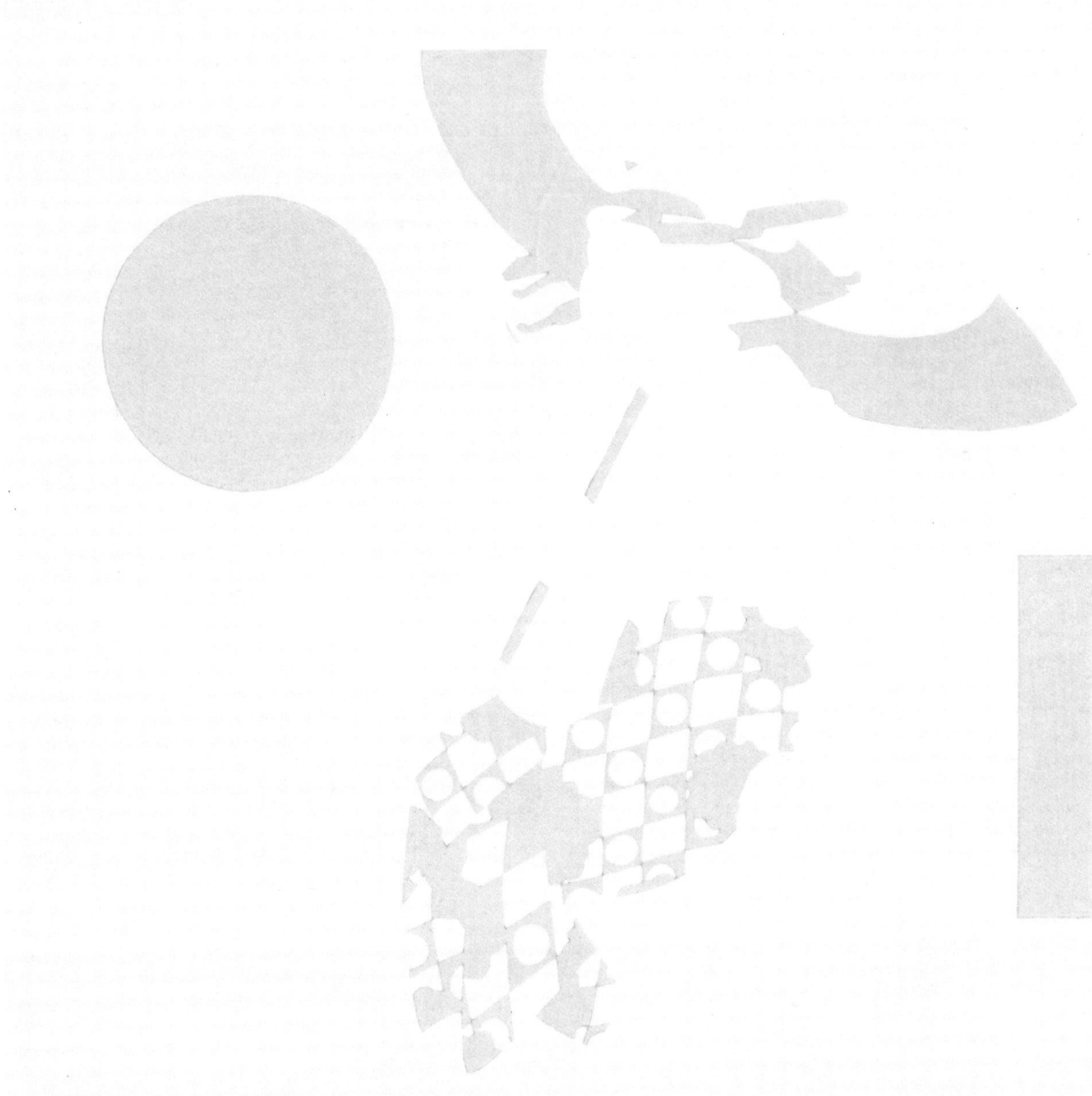

    Pale yellow impression.

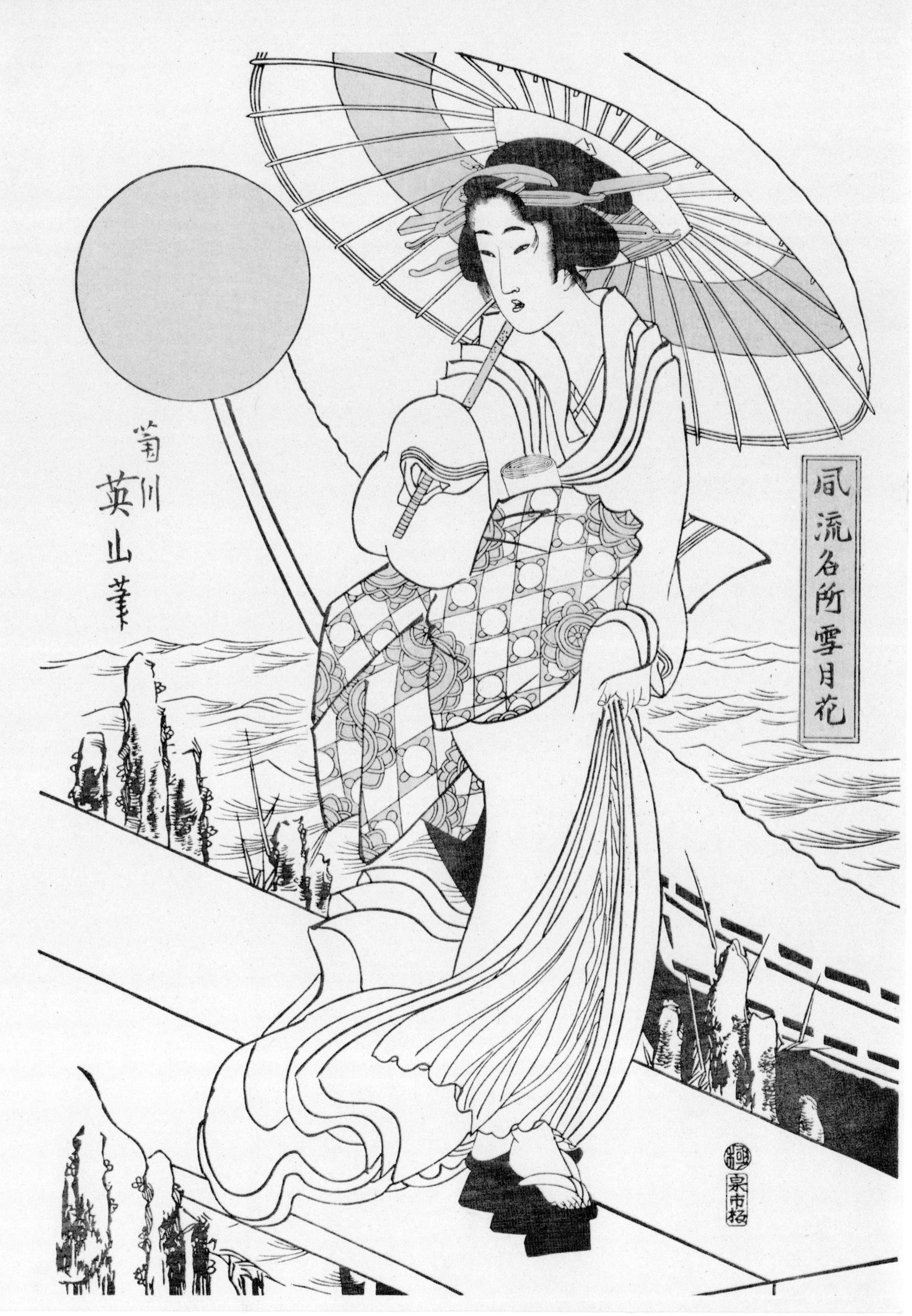
菊川
英山筆
風流名所雪月花
泉市板

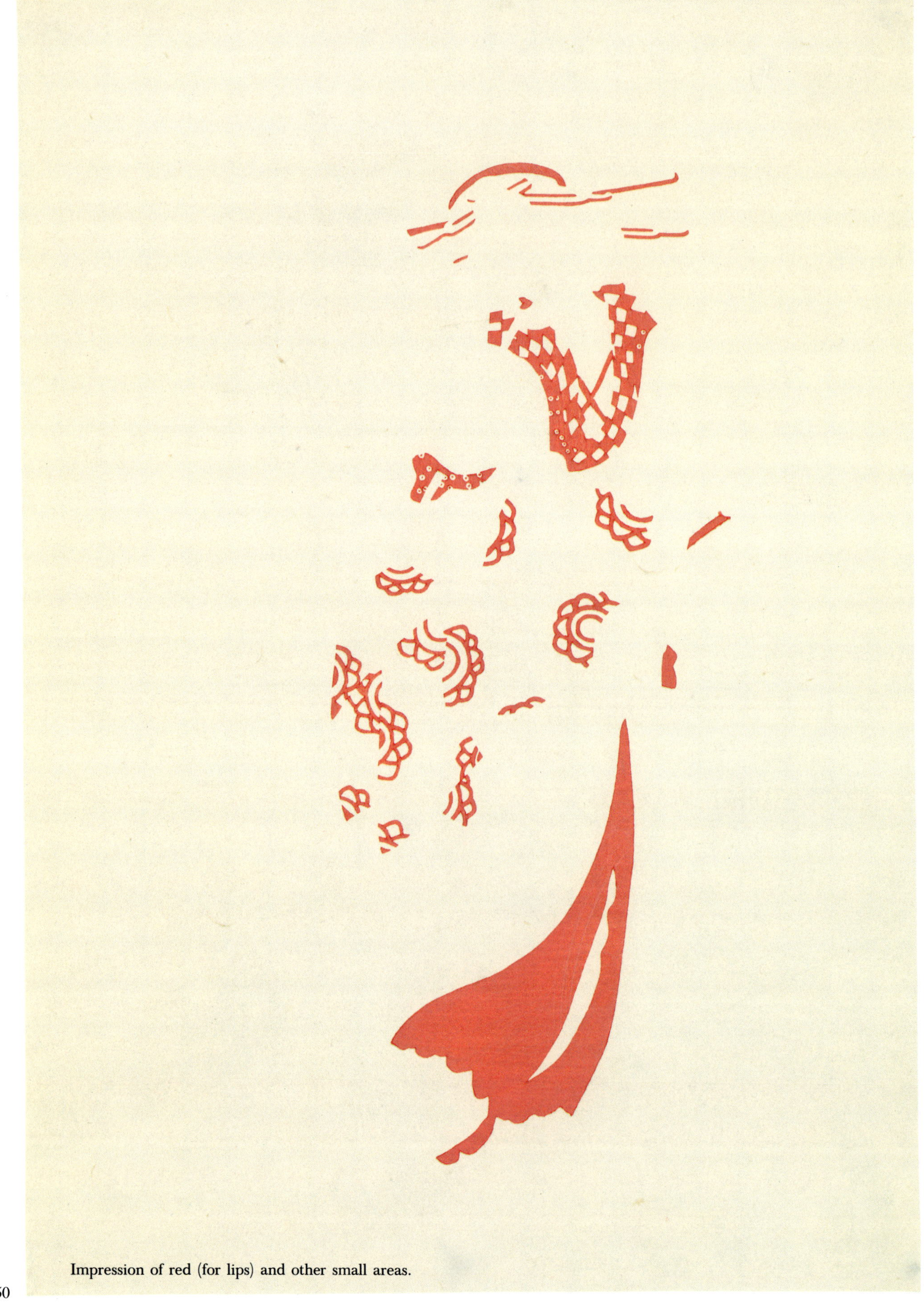

Impression of red (for lips) and other small areas.

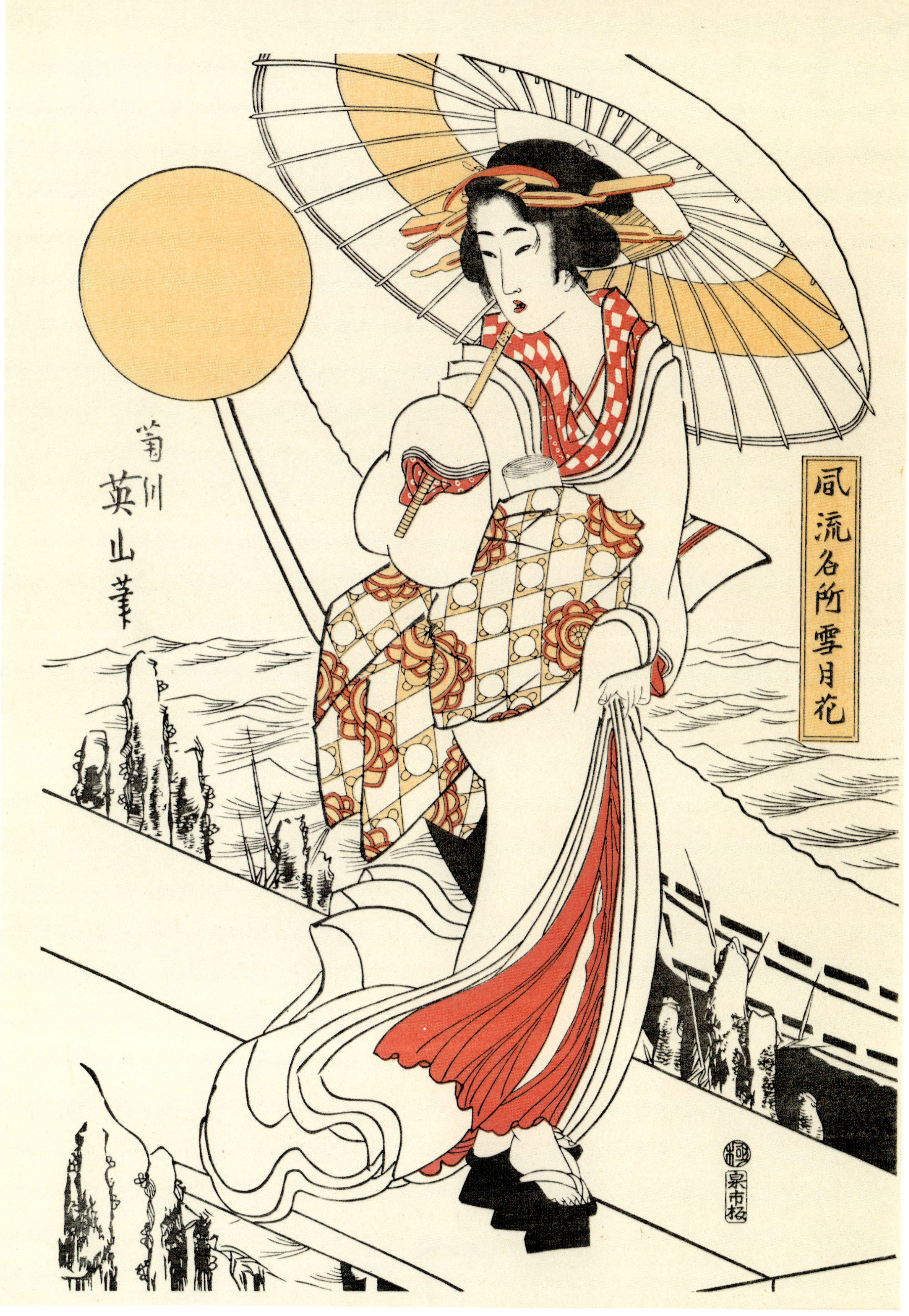

51

Pale red impression.

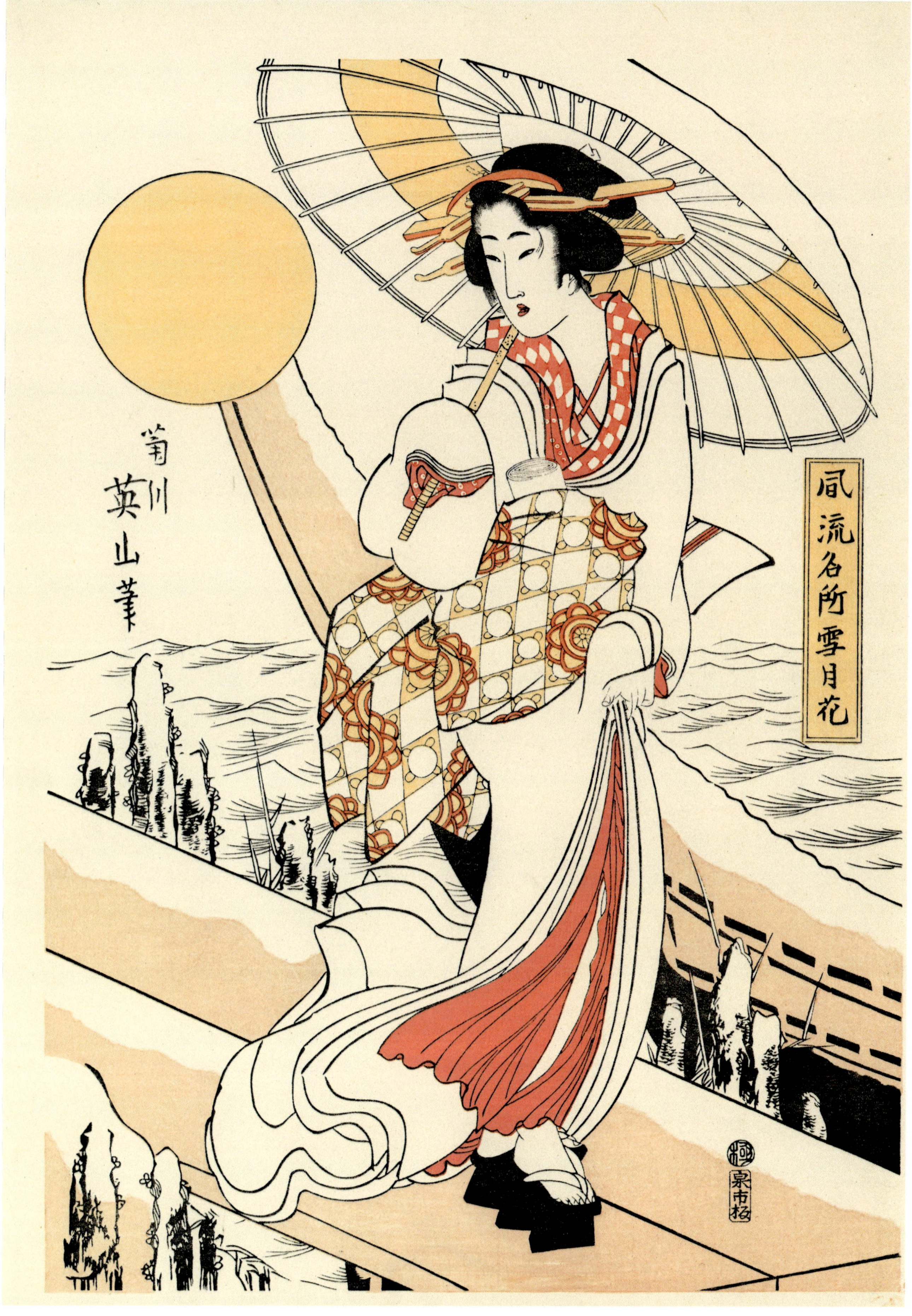
菊川
英山筆
風流名所雪月花

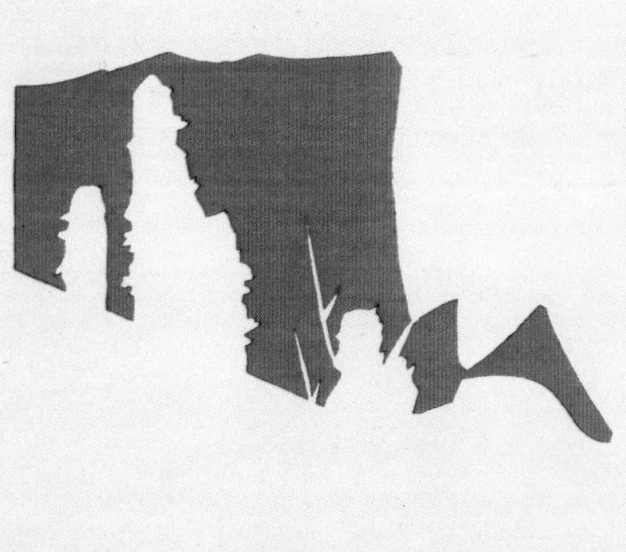
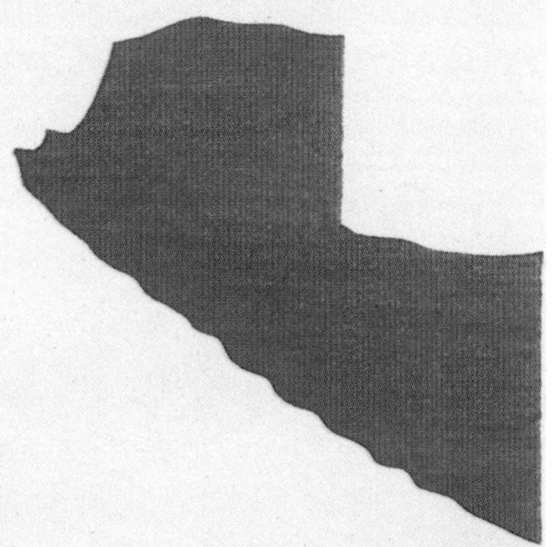

Blue impression.

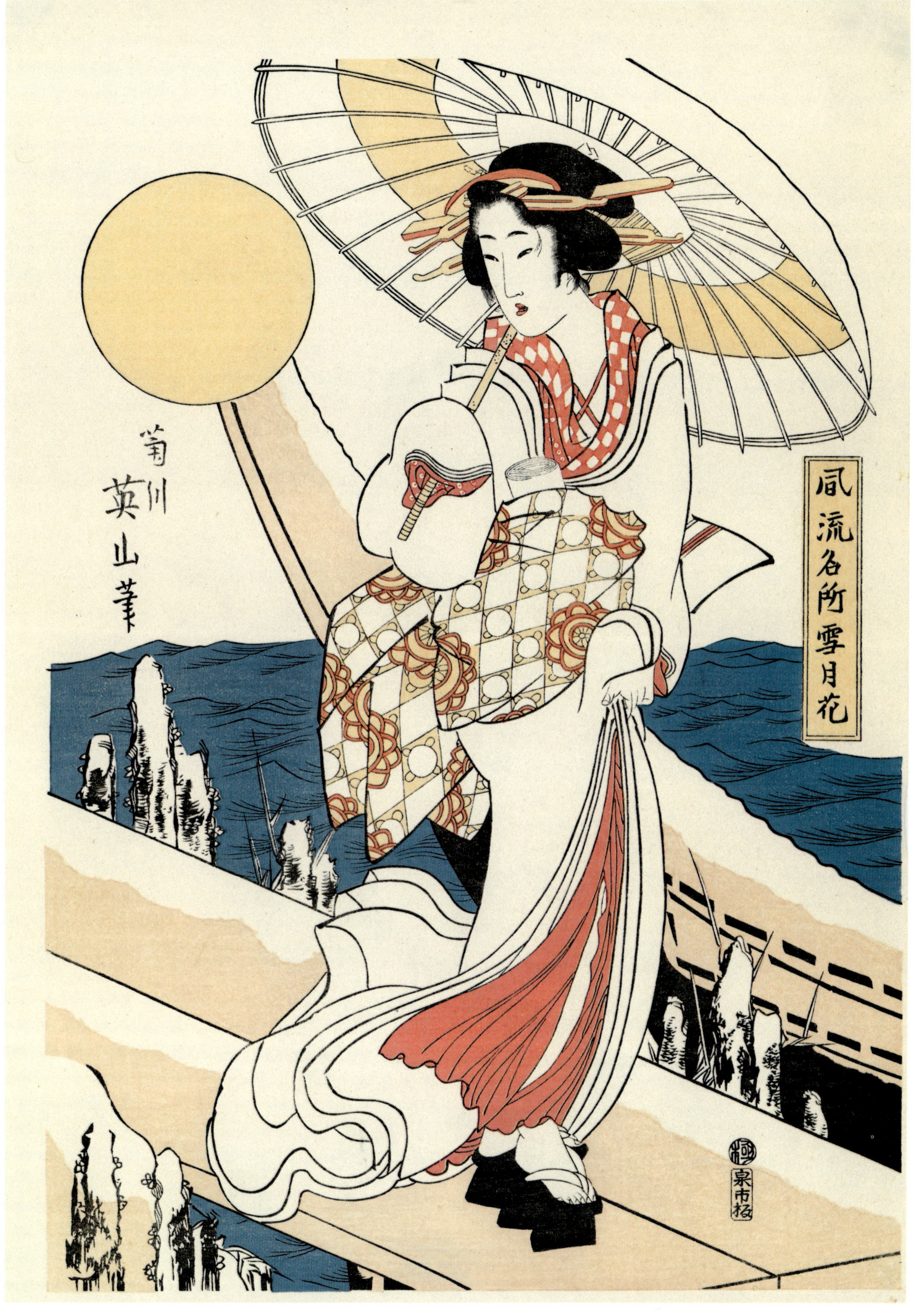

菊川英山筆
風流名所雪月花

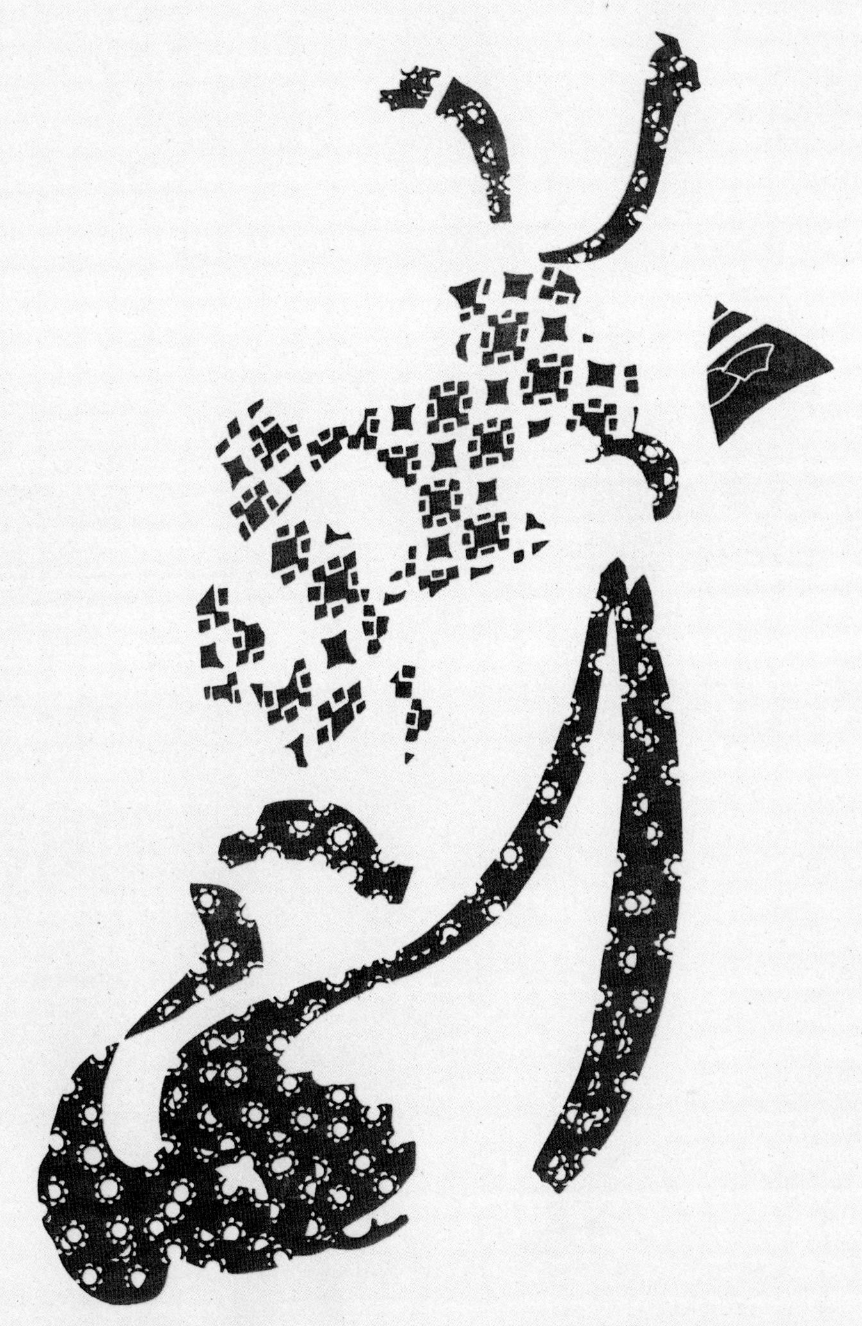

Dark green impression.

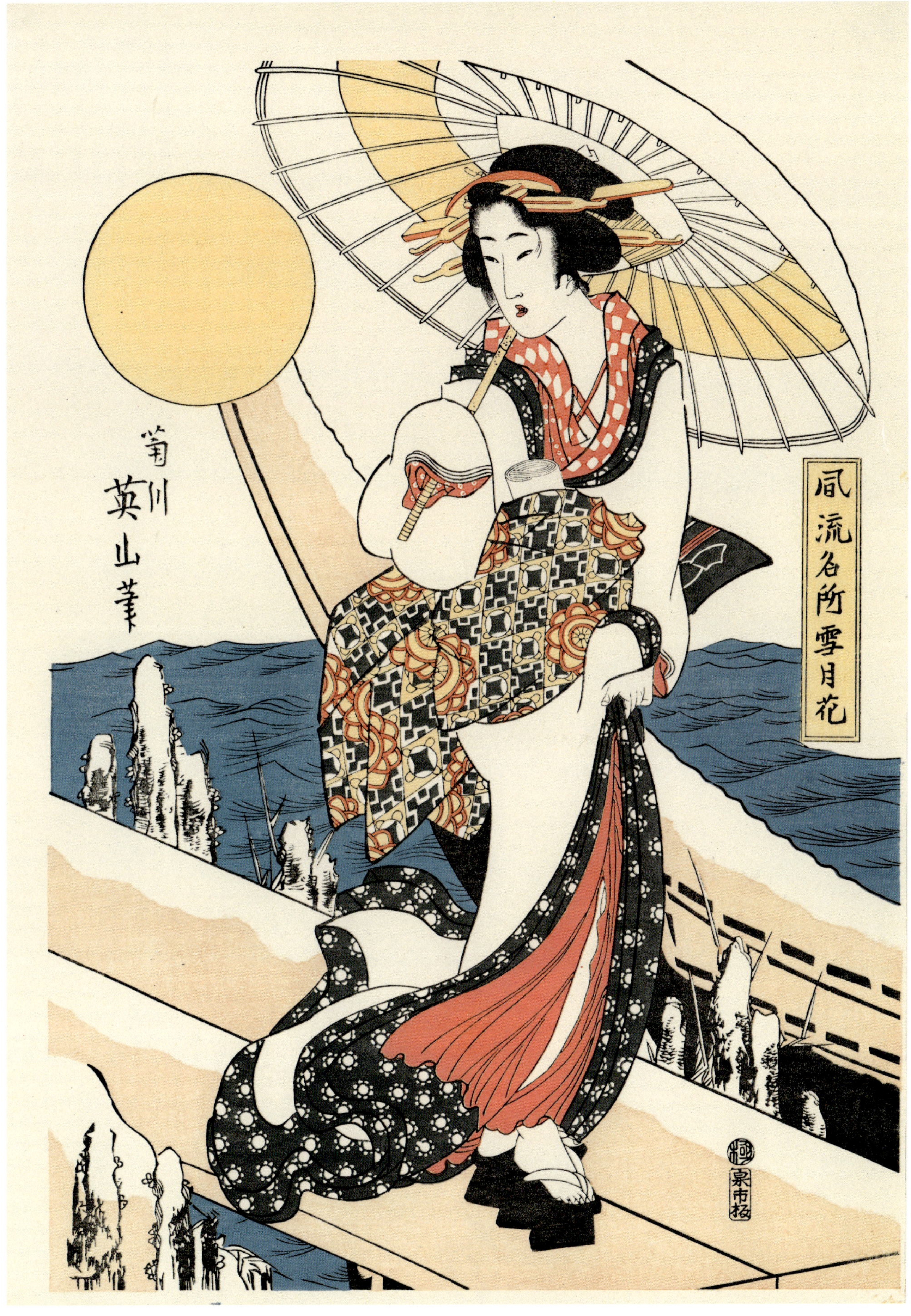
菊川
英山筆
風流名所雪月花

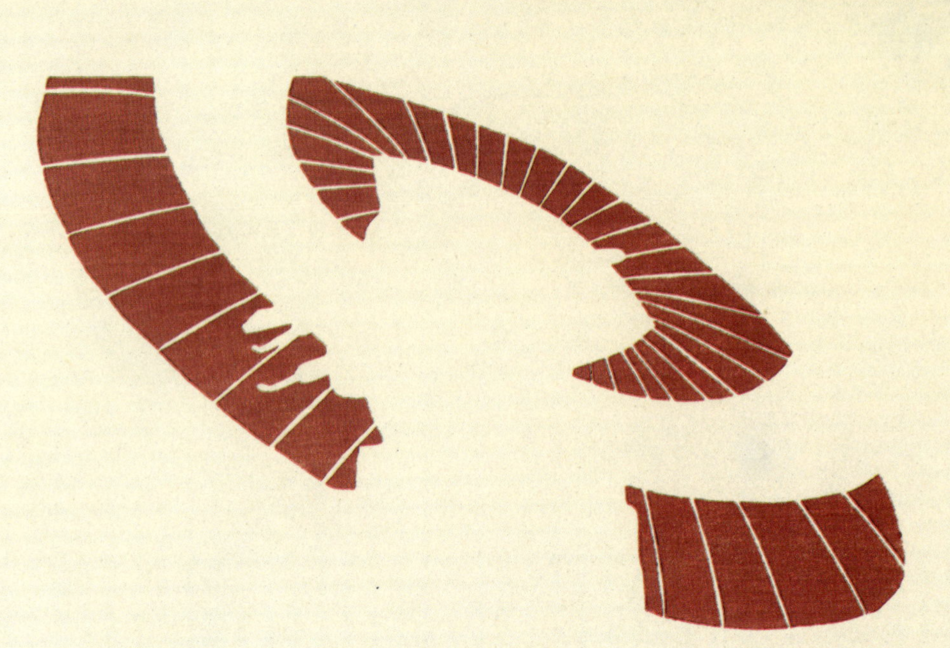

Dark red; this impression was taken off of a different section of
the same woodblock as for blue.

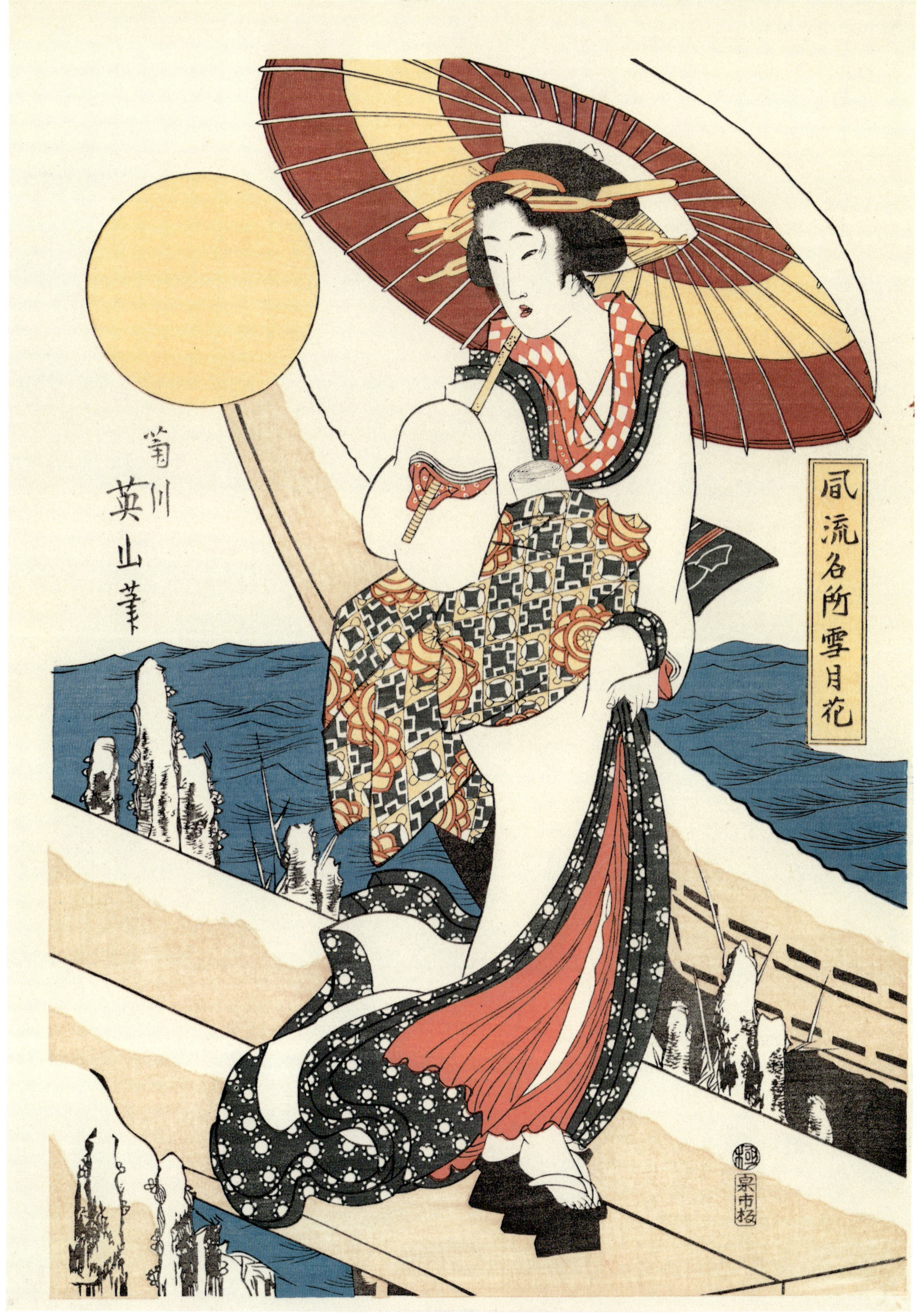

菊川英山筆
風流名所雪月花

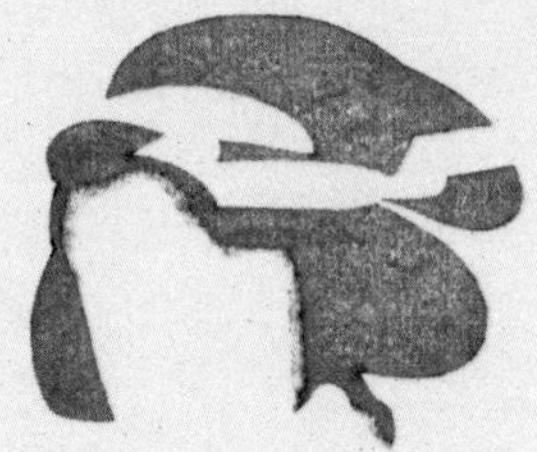

Impression for the grey-black used to intensify the black of the hair by hiding the white of the paper (final lines representing the strands of hair are yet to come).

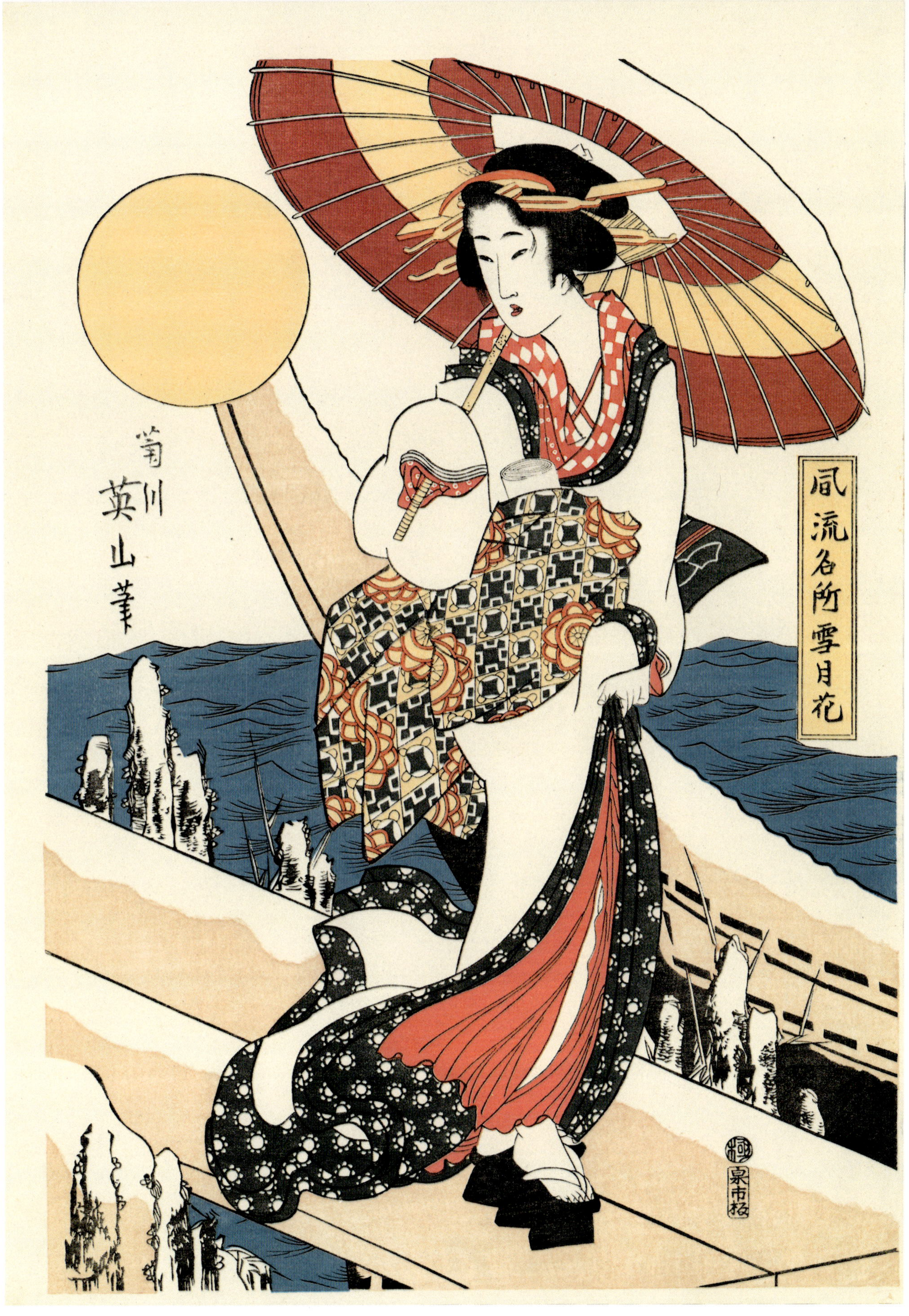

菊川英山筆
風流名所雪月花

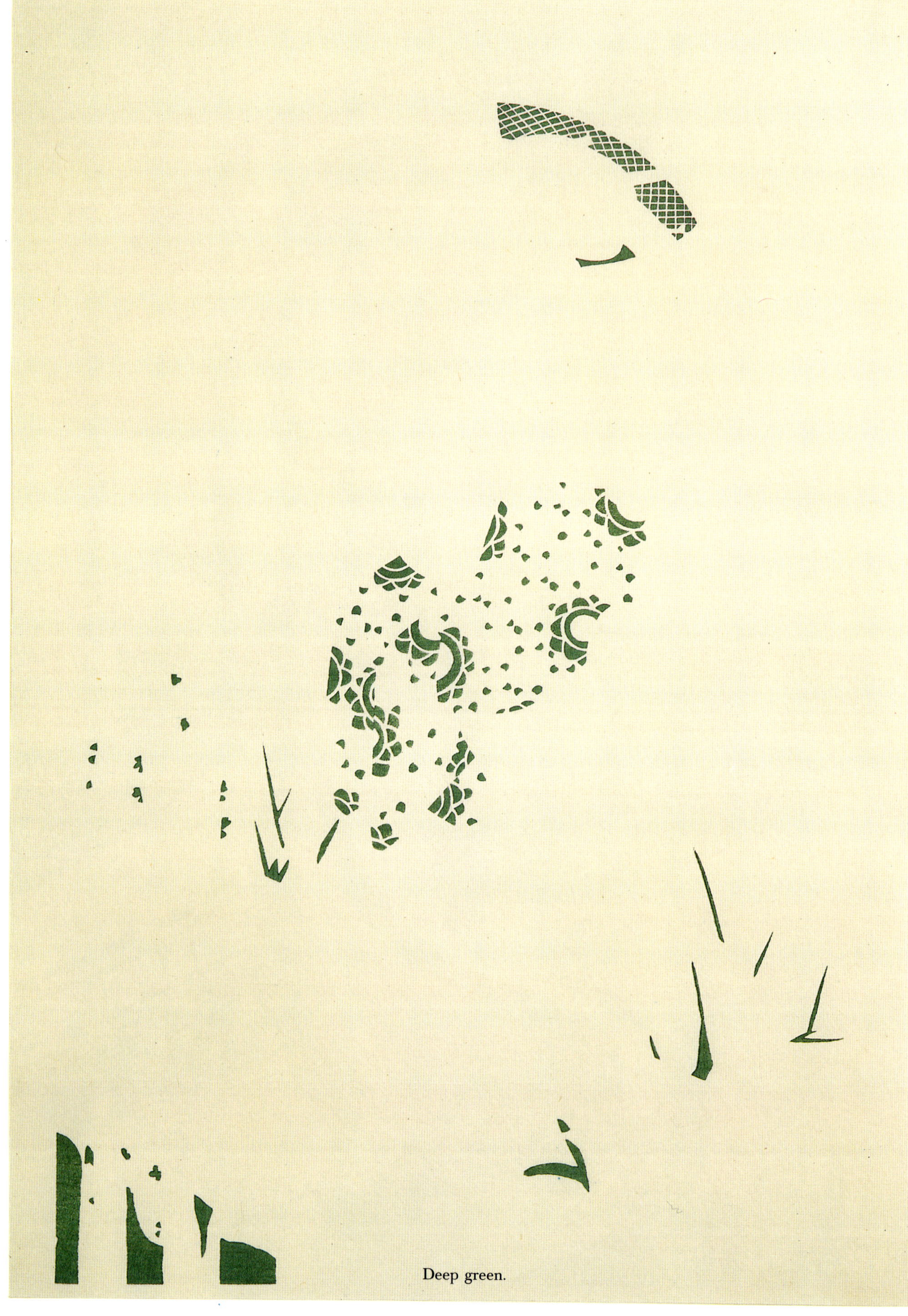

Deep green.

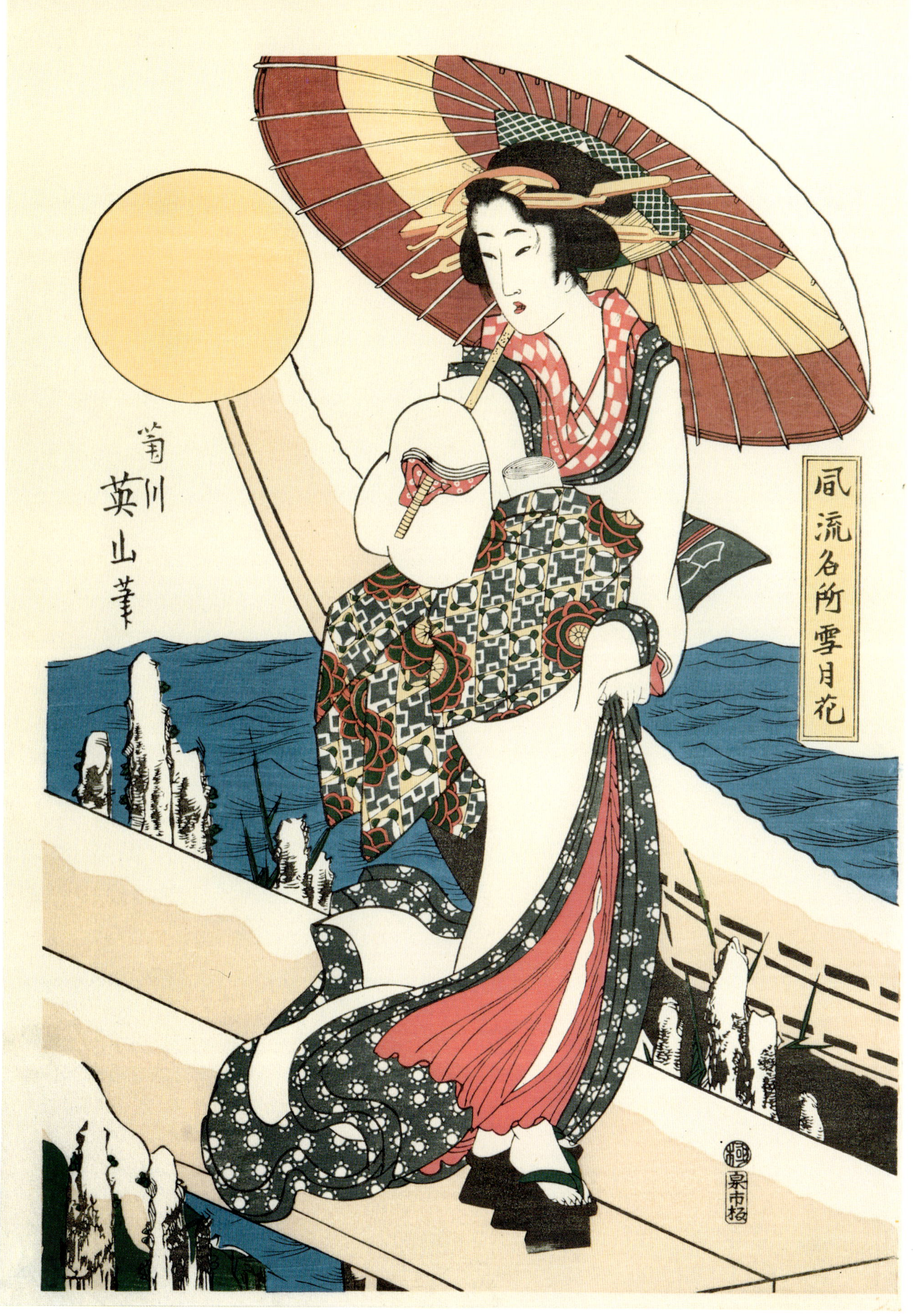
菊川
英山筆
風流名所雪月花

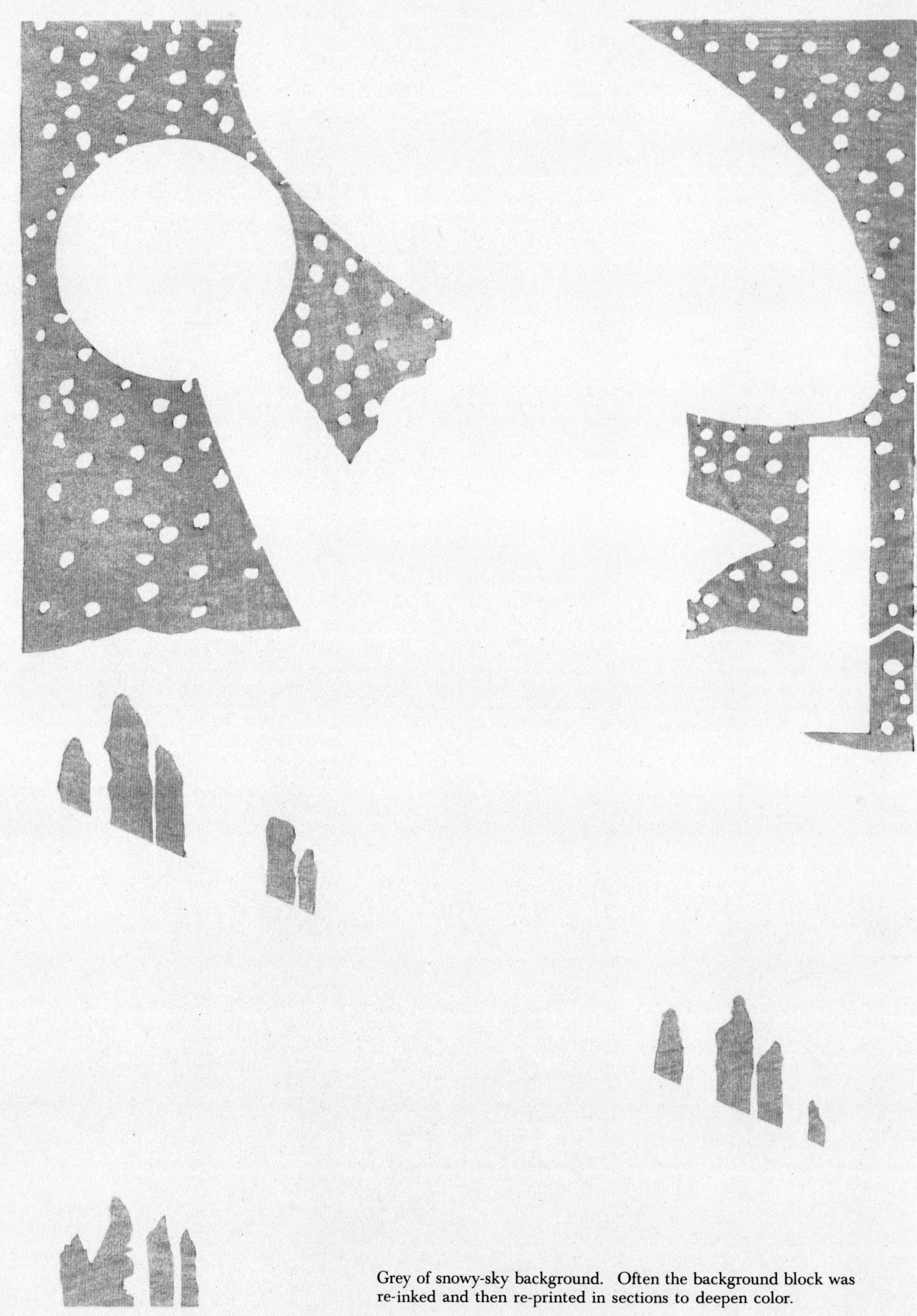

Grey of snowy-sky background. Often the background block was
re-inked and then re-printed in sections to deepen color.

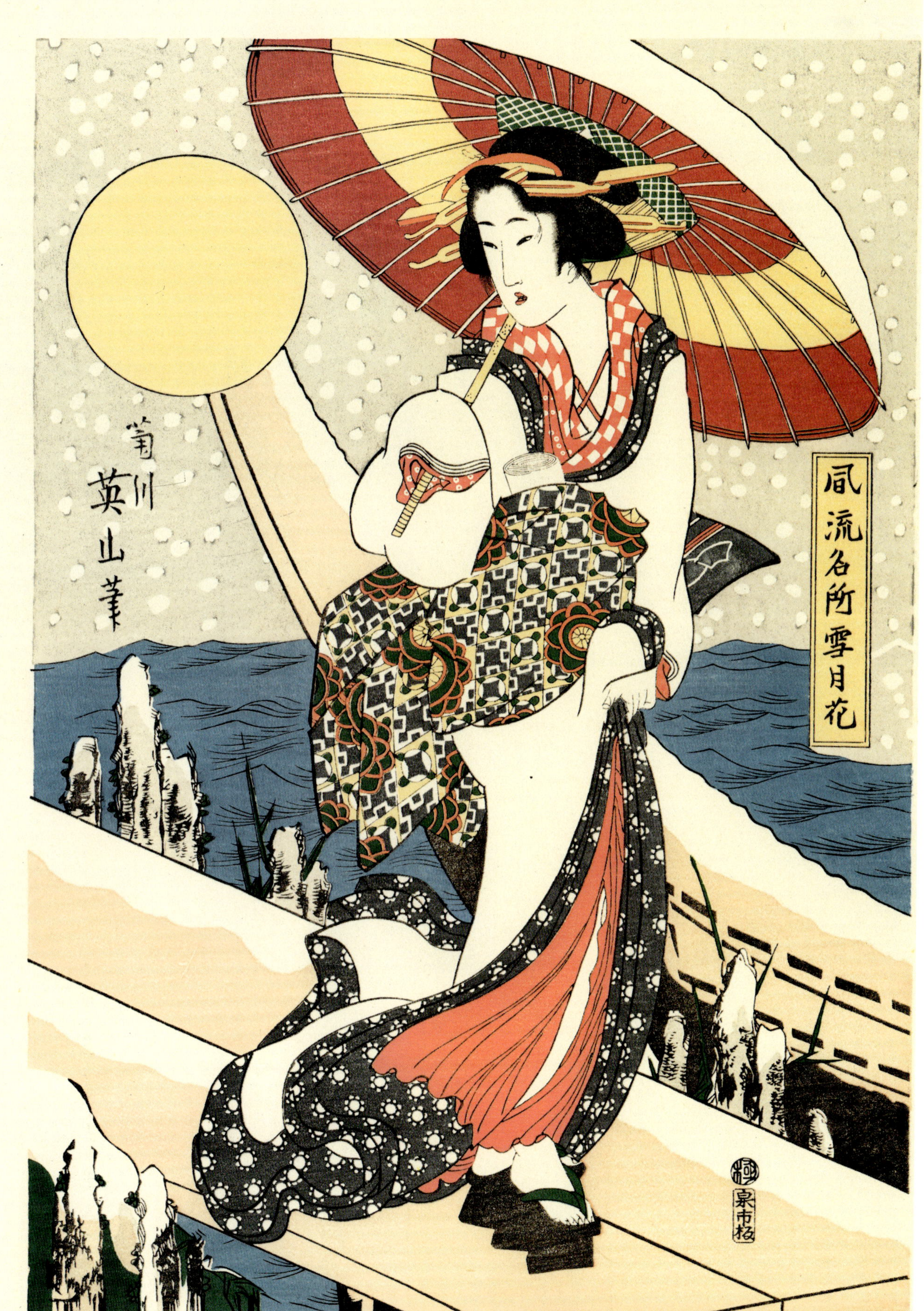
菊川
英山筆
風流名所雪月花

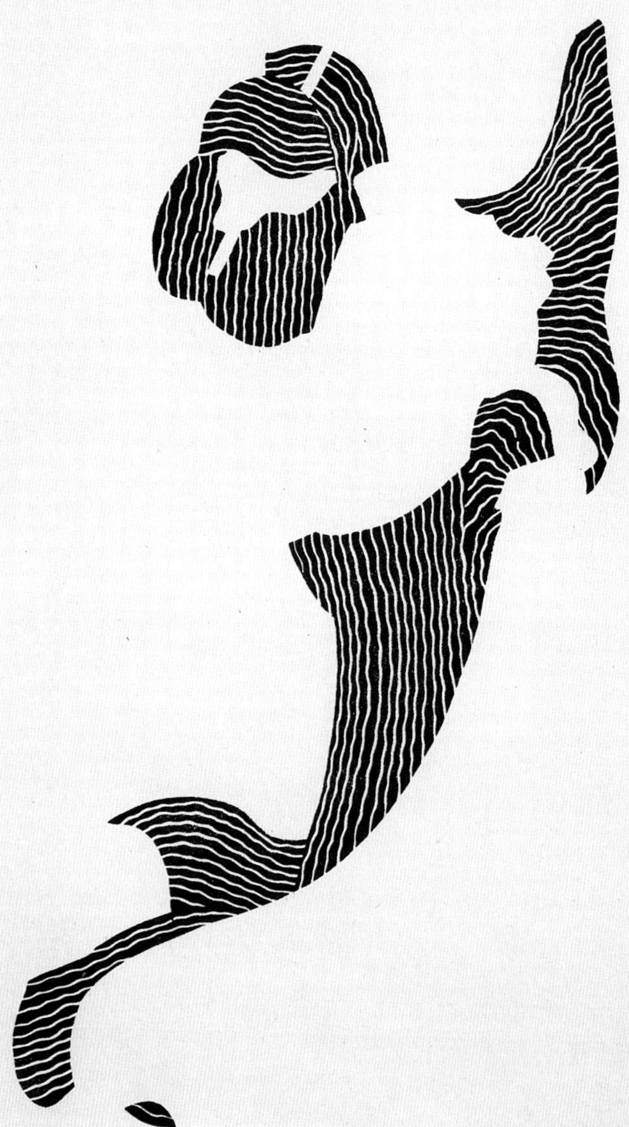

66   Black impression for kimono.

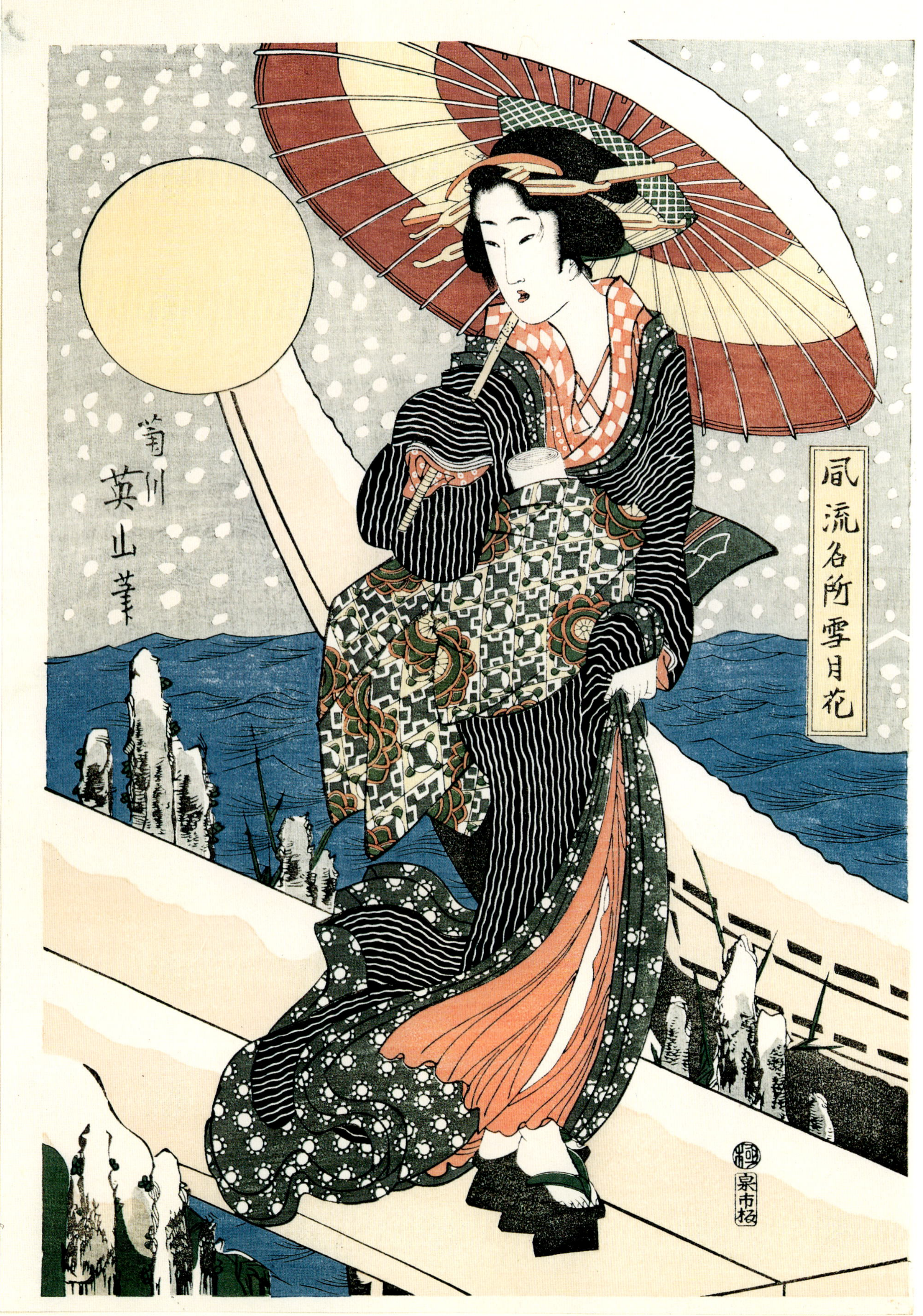

菊川
英山筆
風流名所雪月花

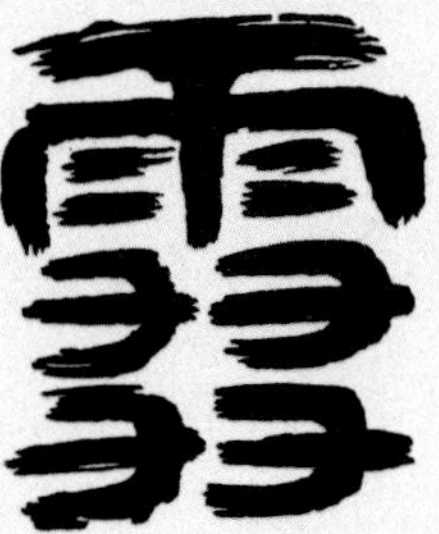 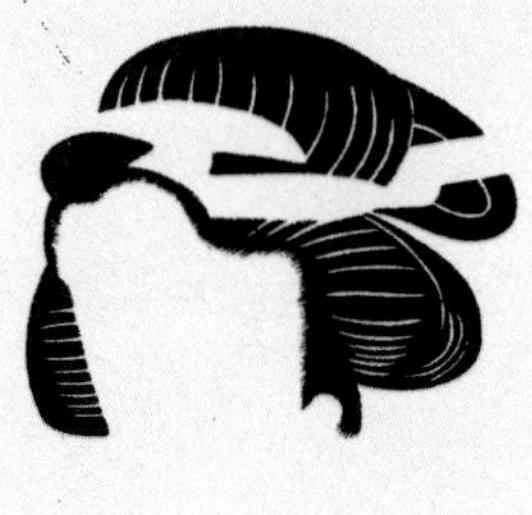

Finishing block impression for the black hair and including the
eye-catching archaic character for "snow."

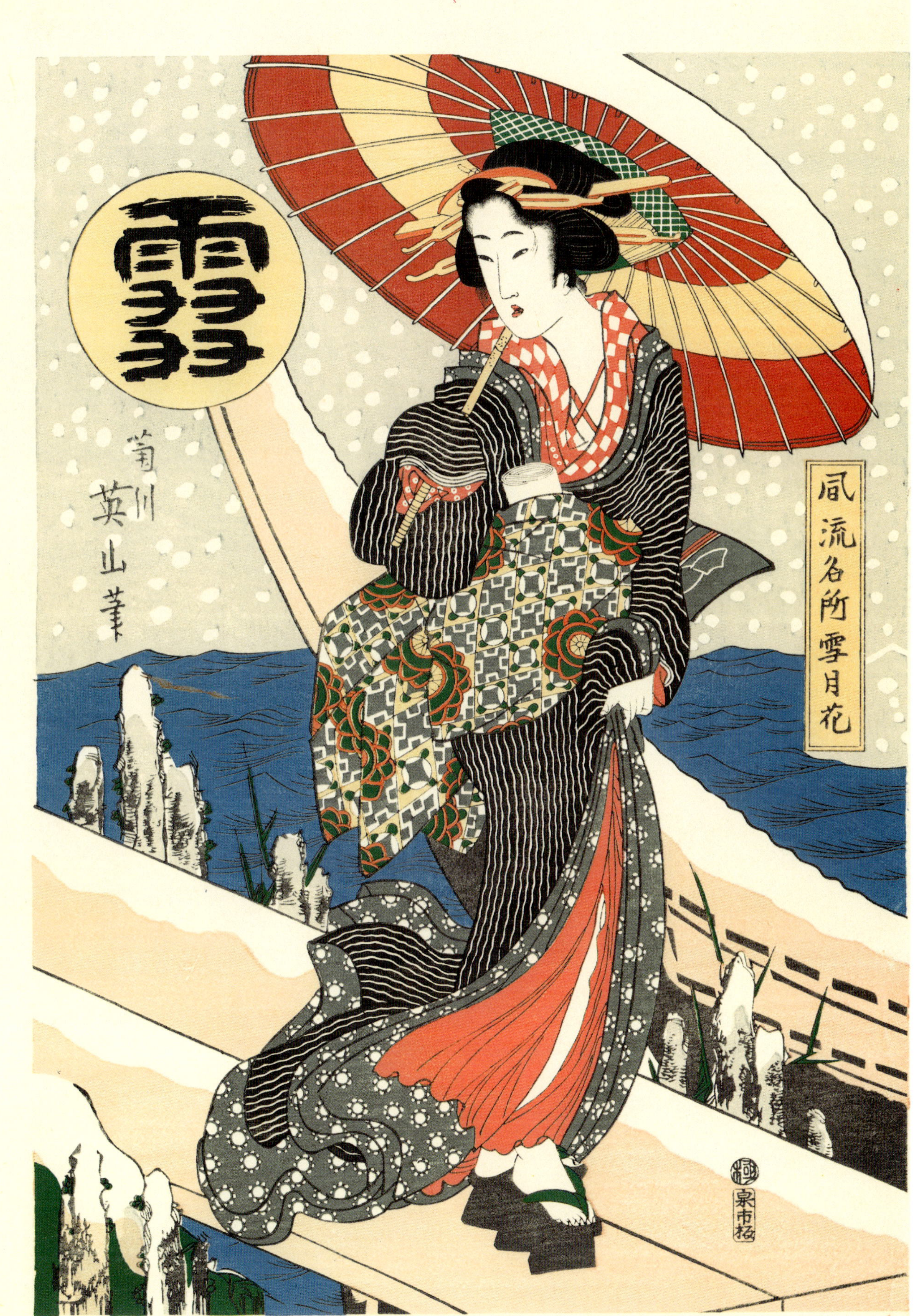
雪
菊川
英山筆
風流名所雪月花

Final black intensifier block impression which results in the
finished full-color print.

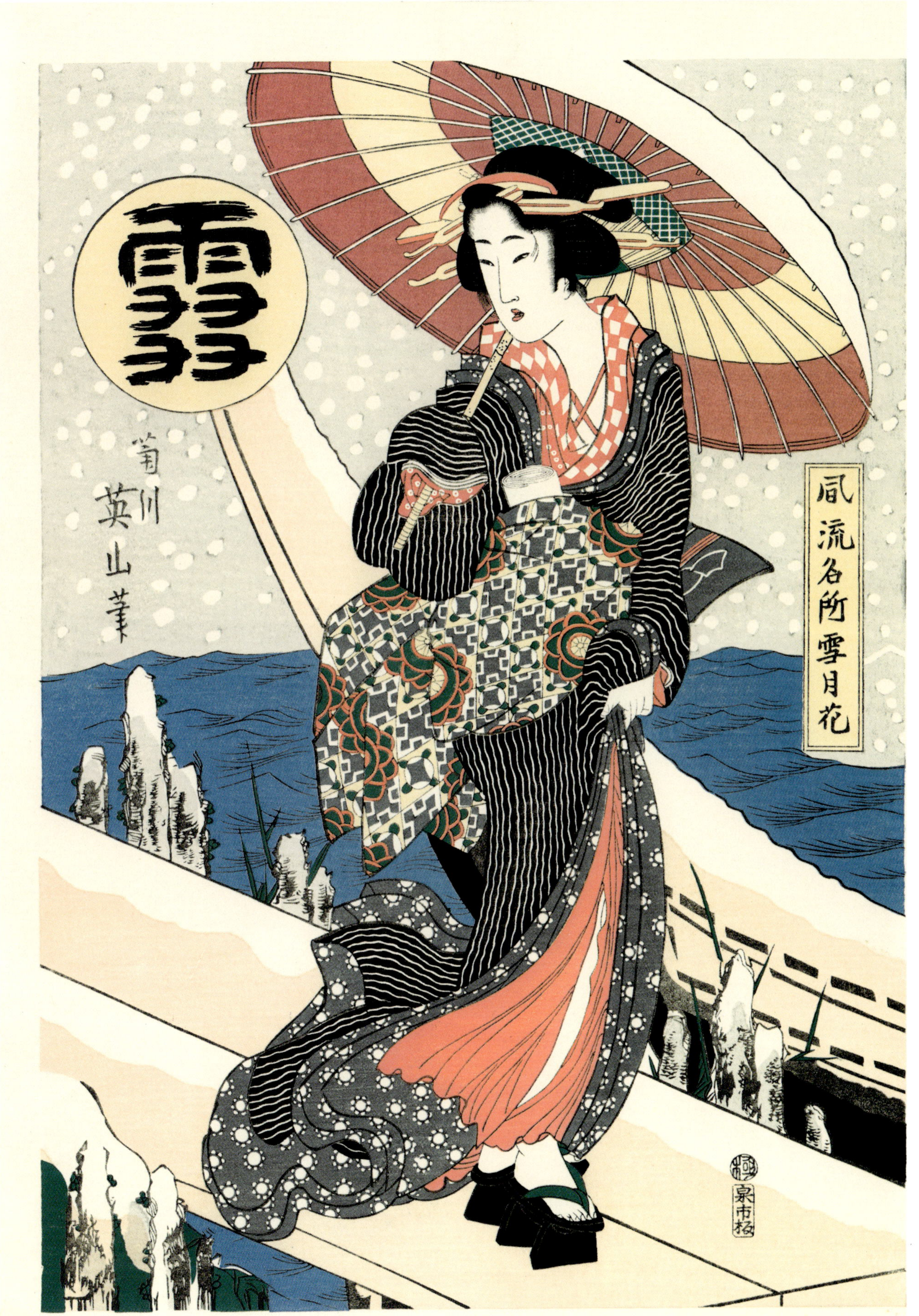

雪
菊川英山筆
風流名所雪月花

Trimming the Finished Print

In the last step of the printmaking process the printer or assistants trimmed and evened the margins around the finished prints (see 1880 print, p. 6). This cut off any stray marks of the *kentō*. Late *nishiki-e* prints often had one or two thin printed black-lines all the way around the composition to delineate the printed area from the unprinted margins. (Over the years many old prints have been mounted or further trimmed to spruce up tattered edges. The margins and even these framing outlines have long since disappeared.) The printer then bundled and tied single-sheet prints and sent them off to the publisher for sale.

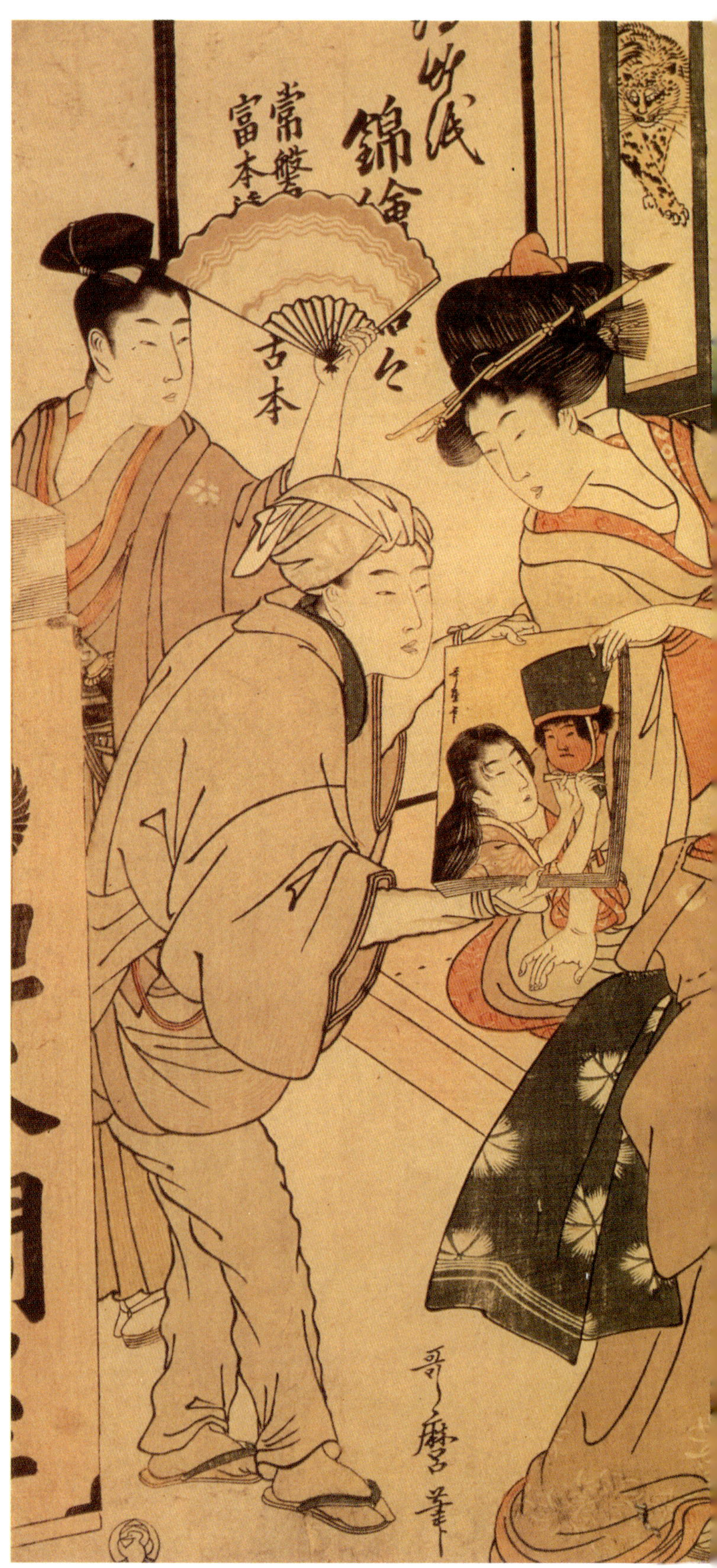

The final two prints from Utamaro's "Making Edo's Famous Souvenir the Full-color Print: Shown as a Parody of Rice Cultivation" ca 1800. Full-color, *ōban* size. The British Museum.

At right the continuation of the scene of printing finds new prints in bundles arriving at the publisher's shop front. They are displayed for sale on racks or hung up. Pictures mounted as hanging scrolls probably are prints too. Stacks of popular fiction books are also offered for sale. At left, subtitled "Distributing the Newest Prints; Autumn Harvest," customers examine "the latest" Utamaro print (which resembles one from late 1790's). Tsuruya ("the House of Crane") depicted here ranks with Nishimuraya (p. 16) and Tsutaya (p. 26) as the leading Edo publishers.

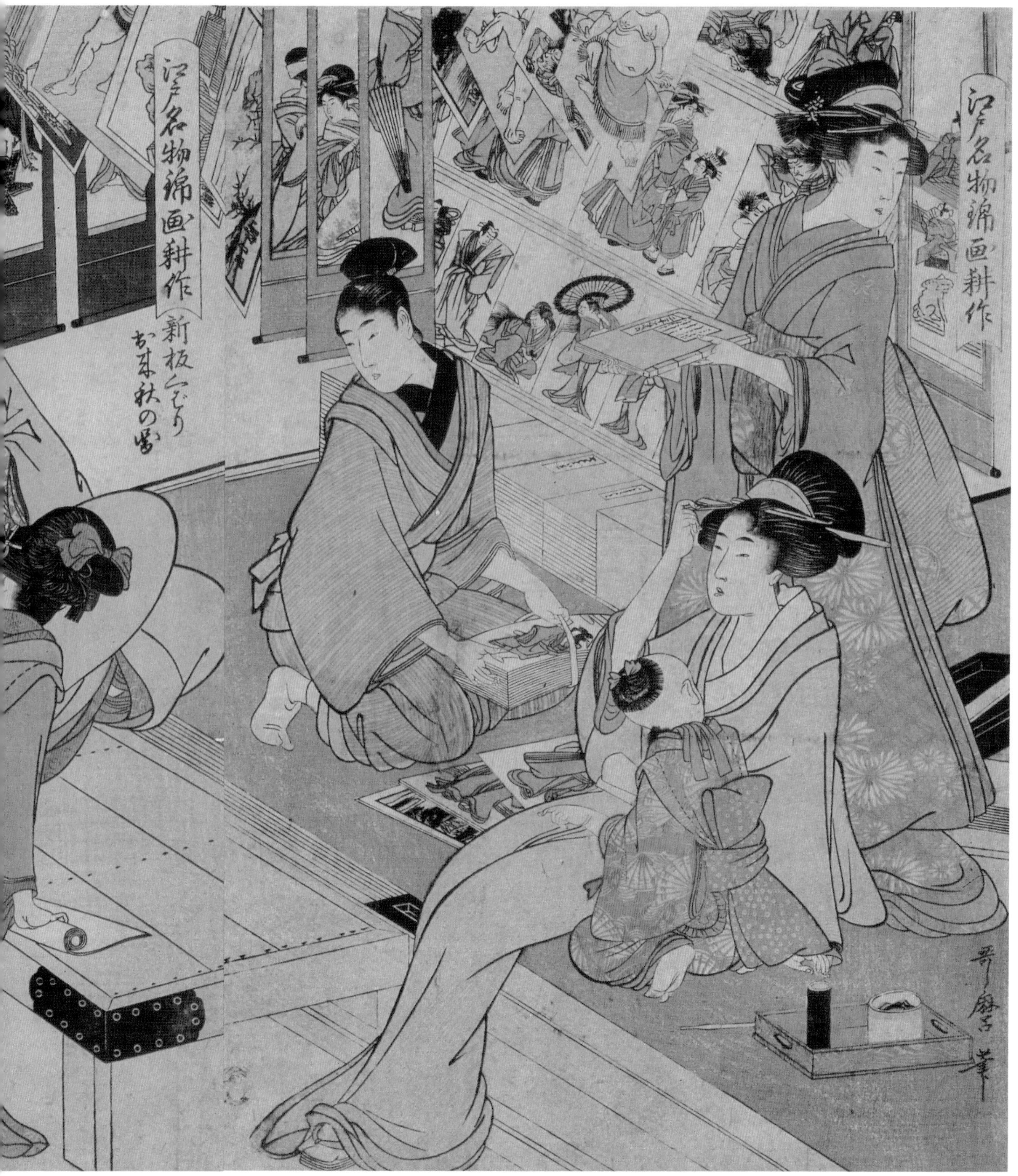

江戸名物錦画耕作
新板にしき
おもと秋の富
江戸名物錦画耕作
哥麿筆

Selling the Prints

Publishers aimed most illustrated books of popular fiction, and many newly designed single-sheet
prints, to go on sale at the New Year's season.

The publisher displayed his wares in piles, mounted on racks, or strung up prints along the open
storefront of his shop, under the short *noren* curtain with his distinctive shop logo. Long and narrow placards advertised recently published or
forthcoming book titles and print series. The publisher also contracted with roving middlemen-

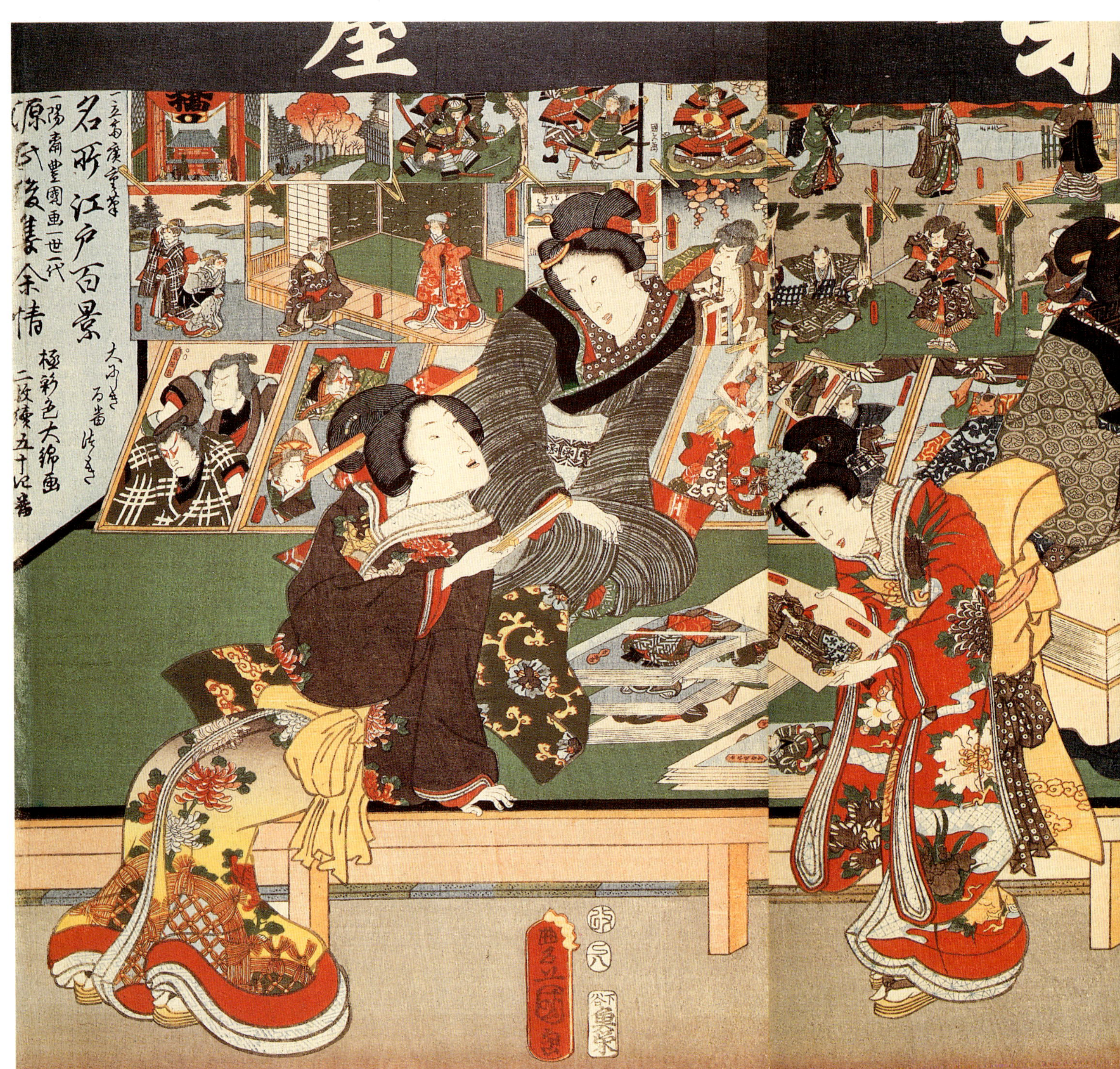

sellers, who supplied smaller shops and open-air street vendors, and with travelling book lenders, to purvey his latest publications. (See also Kiyonaga's print, p. 16). Some prints produced in Edo went on sale in Kamigata and provincal cities.

Three sheets of Kunisada's "Parody of Samurai, Farmers, Artisans, and Merchants in the Latest Fashions: Merchants," 1857. Full-color, *ōban* prints. Private collection.

This depiction of another publisher's shop-front: the Uoya, dates a generation after Utamaro's composition (pp. 72–3), and finds placards advertising (naturally) the latest works of Kunisada (Toyokuni III). The compositions and action poses of the Kunisada-style prints on display reflect the change in taste at the end of the Edo period. On the banner at right the prominent characters announce "*Azuma* [Edo] *Nishiki-e*," the ever popular term for full-color prints. On the center print we find the master blockcarver's name (Yokokawa Chōchiku) included.

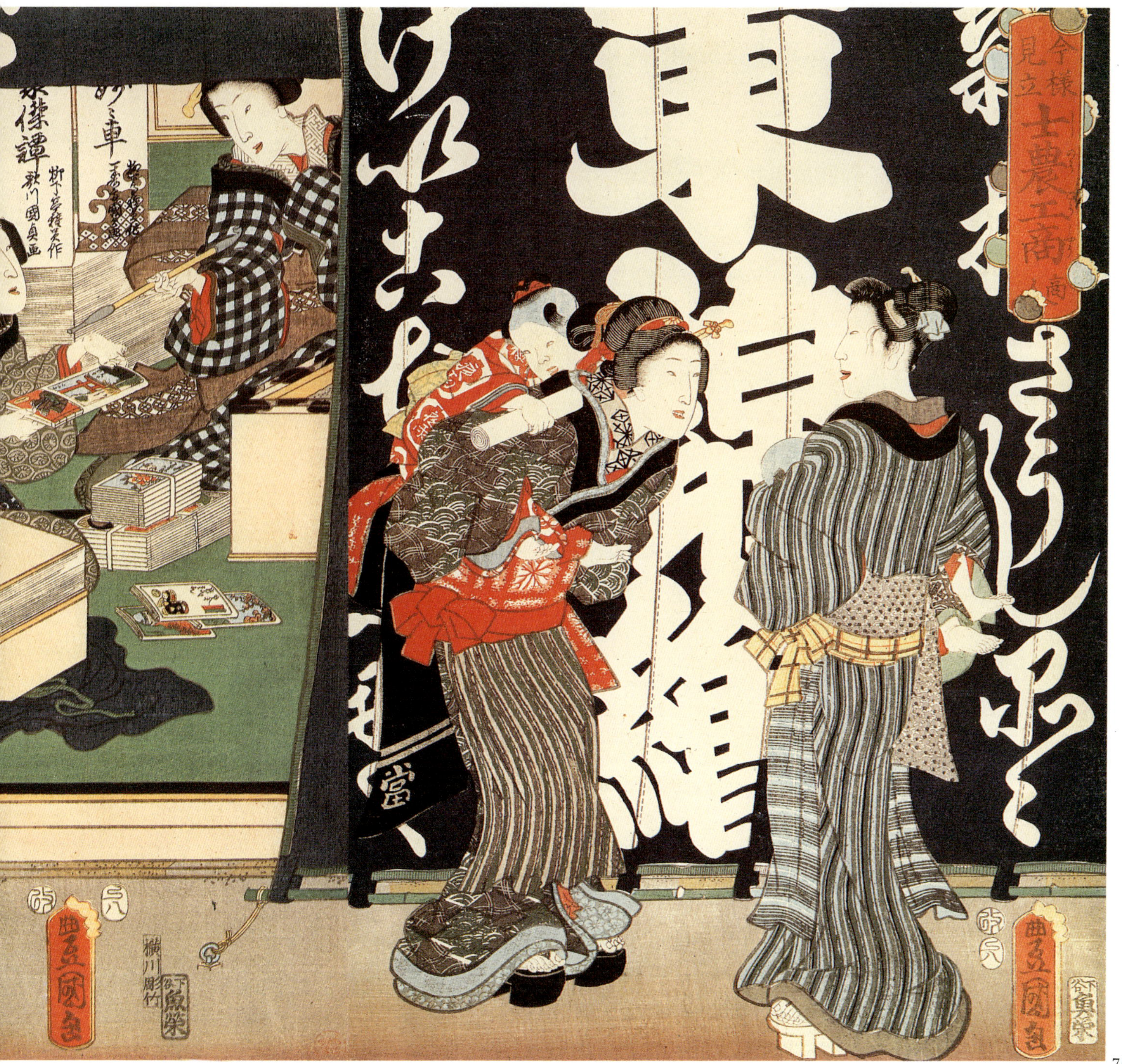

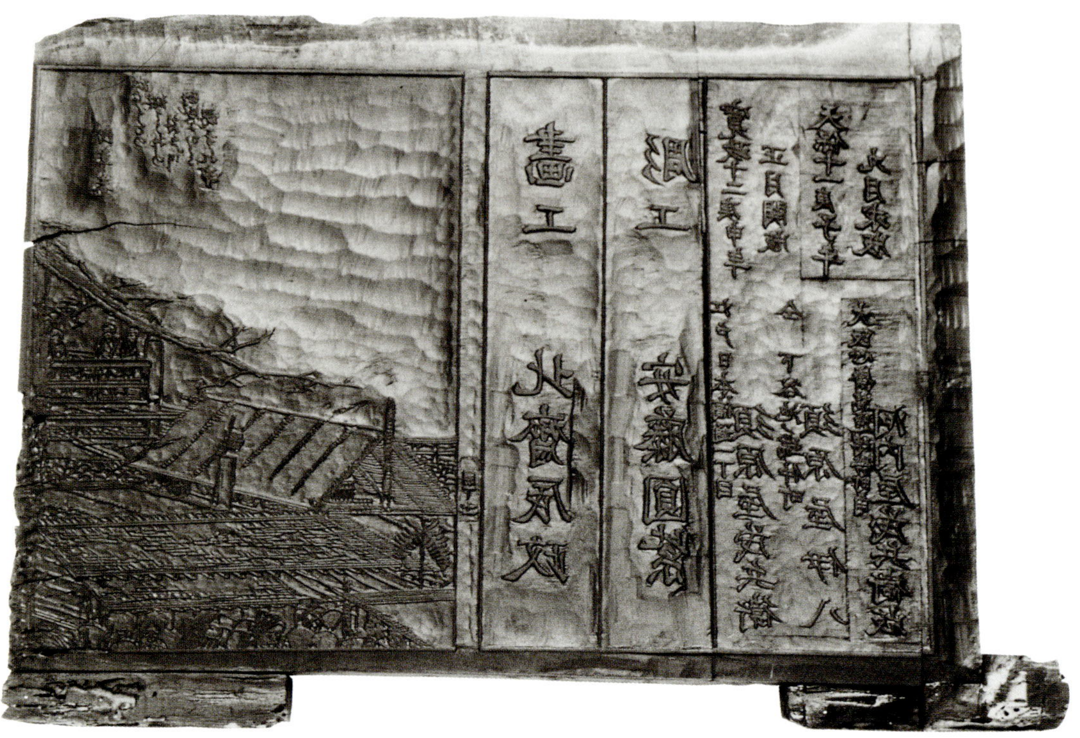

Extant woodblock for the final two pages of the book, "Famous Sights of the Eastern Capital" (*Tōto shōkei ichiran*), illustrated by Hokusai. Last section of the end-page (at right in photo) was re-plugged in 1840. Block originally carved in 1801. Large crack and insect damage visible at left. The Boston Museum of Fine Arts (courtesy of TBS).

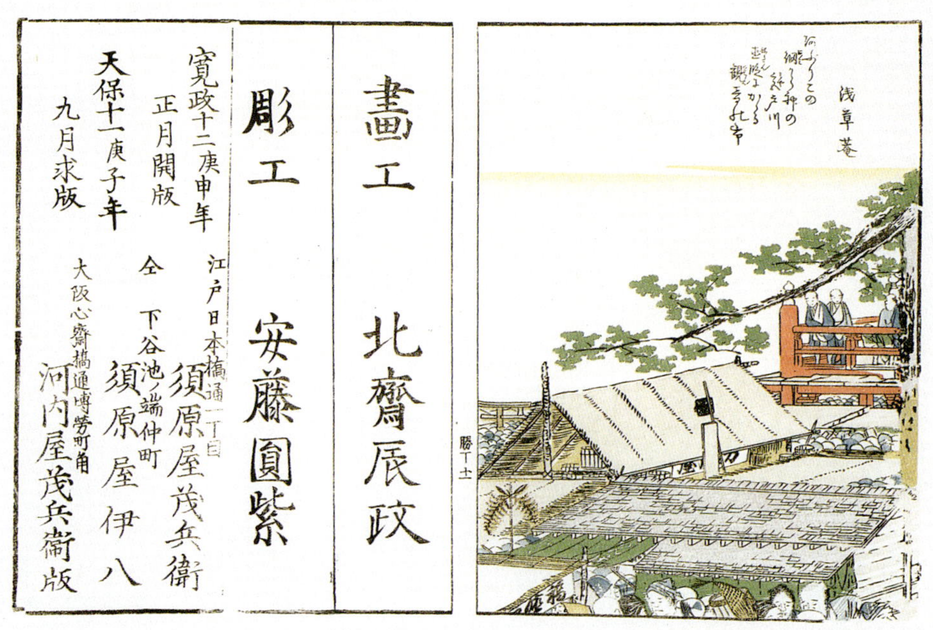

Modern print made off the old woodblock (above) for the last illustration and end-page of "Famous Sights of the Eastern Capital." (Read from r. to l.) after the temple scene at Asakusa (and *kyōka* poem) come the names of the artist: HOKUSAI Tatsumasa, the master carver: Andō Enshi, two earlier publishers: Suharaya Mohei and Suharaya Ihachi, and the last publisher (with date of 1840): Kawachiya Mohei, of Osaka.

The Fate of the Woodblocks

Possesion of the carved woodblocks was in effect the Edo publisher's sole means of holding "copyright" on his prints and publications. Little is known about where or for how long the publisher warehoused the bulky blocks. The *sumi* used on keyblock and text woodblocks served to preserve the wood somewhat from insects and rot. Most woodblocks, especially the keyblocks, had a wood flange and cap bracing usually on the narrower ends against the wood grain in order to ease handling and storage and to help prevent warping. In the 19th century this traditional method was replaced by wood slats affixed to the ends. They served the same functions. A 19th-century record says the slats were often slightly wider than the thickness of the blocks which prevented the scratching of block faces when stored. Even with such reinforcement, a block could warp or crack virtually overnight. The fickle Edo public however, proved by far the biggest threat to the useful life of a woodblock. Unlike serious books, most full-color prints and works of popular fiction had only a brief season before they went out of demand. The woodblocks, as mentioned, were frequently re-used on the back or planed down and recarved.

On the other hand, a popular book illustrated by Hokusai provides evidence of extensive selling and buying of woodblocks in the early 19th century, and of full-color illustrations in enough demand to warrant republication several times over a span of 40 years. The work, entitled *Famous Sights of the Eastern Capital*, consists of satirical poems (*kyōka*) with full-color illustrations by Hokusai of Edo scenes on every page. In addition to various editions of the book, the complete set of 107 woodblocks (including 4 for the book jackets) has recently come to light at the Boston Museum of Fine Arts, where the set survives thanks to the efforts of a late 19th-century *ukiyo-e* collector, William S. Bigelow.

Tsutaya Jūsaburō's name follows that of the artist, Hokusai, and the master blockcarver, Andō Enshi, on the end-page of the first edition in 1800.

The publisher must, in actuality, have been Jūsaburō II, heir of the famous Jūsaburō who had died in 1797. Almost immediately, a consortium of 3 publishers (including Tsutaya) brought out the book again from the same blocks but with the publisher's names re-written and plugged into the woodblock for the end-page. In 1815 the woodblocks had been sold to a Nagoya publisher, Hishiya Kimbei, who plugged in his name and date, in place of Tsutaya's, in the plug already set into the block for the end-page. One of the keyblocks in the set had apparently cracked because the page was recarved on the back of a woodblock (also by strange coincidence still extant, but in Leiden) for another book illustrated by Hokusai. By 1840 the blocks, worn but still printable, had changed hands again. This time the publisher, Kawachiya Mohei, lived in Osaka. He again had to have that one keyblock recarved since it apparently had already gone from the set. He plugged in the 1840 date, and his name and address, replacing Hishiya Kimbei on the end-page block, which is extant in Boston showing this final (plugged) stage. (See photos at l.). The episode suggests how the public in cities outside of the capital had a lively interest in visual images of Edo, and how publishers were indeed able to make profits by re-printing off old woodblocks at least in the 19th century.

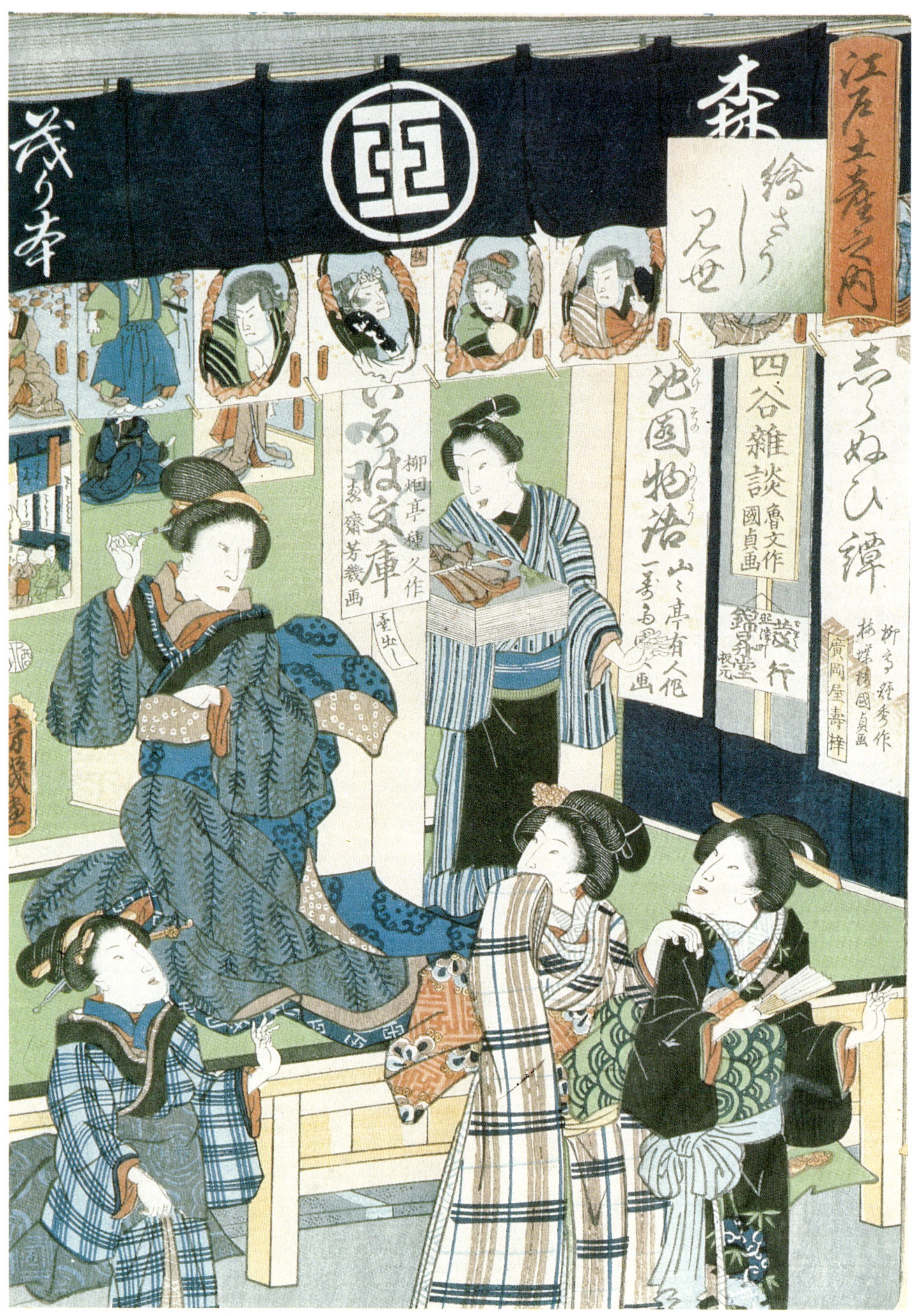
江戸土産之内
森
茂り本
絵さうし
つ世
いろは文庫
柳畑亭種久作
齋芳幾画
池園物語
山々亭有人作
一英斎国輝画
四谷雑談
魯文作
国貞画
志らぬひ譚
廣岡屋壽梓

Full-Color Woodblock Printmaking Today

Despite tremendous changes in the graphic arts with all the new techniques at use in Japan today, the traditional full-color woodblock carving and printing skills continue to be handed down. The hereditary names of lines of craftsmen also continue, although they are all but forgotten except by the individuals involved. In 1978 the Japanese government designated the techniques "intangible important cultural assets" in order to help ensure their preservation. An organization of craftsmen called "The Association for the Preservation of *Ukiyo-e* Woodblock-print Carving and Printing" was established and receives modest government support. In 1987 there were about 16 blockcarvers and 30 master printers with the experience and skills necessary to produce a full-color *ukiyo-e* print working in a half dozen studios located in Tokyo and Kyoto. This compares to the 202 names of master blockcarvers alone recorded at work in Edo in 1852, at the time the old master-apprentice guild system was about to be legally abolished.

For the Eizan print reproduction, "Snow," Itoh Susumu (seen at work in the photos of this book) at age sixty-five recarved the blocks from a photographic reproduction. He is a Tokyo woodblock carver of the main Matsushima line and has followed in the footsteps of his father Chūjirō, who was principal carver for Torii Kiyotada VIII. He has no heir to take over for him. Kajikawa Yoshio (also seen at work) did the printing off the new woodblocks. He too has long been active in efforts to preserve traditional techniques, and has served as head of the Preservation Association. Kajikawa follows in a long line of Reiganjima printers, and expects his son to carry on. Kajikawa has taken over functions of the old-time publisher, such as helping to choose compositions, delegating work to various craftsmen for large projects, and storing the carved woodblocks. Both Kajikawa and Itoh live and work in present-day Bunkyō and Taitō wards in the northern part of Tokyo where printers and woodblock carvers have been established since the Edo period.

Young people, although interested in learning the traditional techniques, are understandably daunted by the years required of an old-style apprenticeship. Moreover, while there are still projects for the experienced carver or printer, there are few of the smaller jobs that brought in a living wage while learning the craft. As one step towards assuring the skills continue in the next generation, the government through the Preservation Association has instituted a system which designates enough funds to support five middle-level apprentices each year for three years. Then master craftsmen must take over. For example, Kajikawa Yoshio provides room, board, and stipend to several apprentice printers for another three years each. Six years is barely enough time to learn the basics. Many of the young men apprenticing this year wonder if there will be projects in the future.

One of the biggest worries today among those seeking to preserve traditional woodblock printmaking is that the lone surviving Tokyo artisan, Shimano Tokusaburō, who knows how to season, cut, and plane the cherry woodboards for the woodblocks, is in his late seventies. His son-in-law, Shintarō, already in his late forties, has agreed to carry on the Tokyo business, but he has yet to establish a reputation among blockcarvers that comes close to that of Tokusaburō's. Moreover he sees no younger people interested in learning the craft.

The making of modern copies of old Edo-period prints (by re-cutting the woodblocks or, less commonly, by printing off extant old blocks or plugged blocks) is the work of skilled craftsmen who have retained the old techniques. Unscrupulous art dealers or uninformed antique sellers can sell the unwary collector these modern prints as old "originals." Copies made seventy years ago of "Edo-period" prints have naturally aged and attained a faded look. Copies have also been printed with "already" faded colors. Prints passed off as first editions that are actually from later printings or late 19th century or early 20th century copies undeniably circulate. In questionable works, modern substitutes used for some pigments, for example for the blues or lavender, rarely have faded as much as would be expected.

Bright blues or lavender in an otherwise old-looking print may indicate a later copy, or that these colored areas have been re-printed to "improve" an old print. A different feel in the weight of the paper or a yellowish cast may be another clue to an early modern copy. The real market in forgeries or re-touched works however, is in *ukiyo-e* paintings not woodblock prints. Japanese dealers and *ukiyo-e* collectors scoff at the idea of there being a problem with copies of *nishiki-e*.

Modern reproductions, as opposed to copies of *ukiyo-e* woodblock prints, produced in the last forty years (*i.e.* the Eizan print used for this book) usually are labeled "reproduction". A label often printed in the margin or on the back gives the names of the woodblock carver, printer, publisher and even papermaker. Sometimes this information is included in a pamphlet which accompanies each print. Because carving the blocks from photographs ensures accurate reproduction down to the smallest detail, as an extra precaution, most contemporary blockcarvers have an agreement to

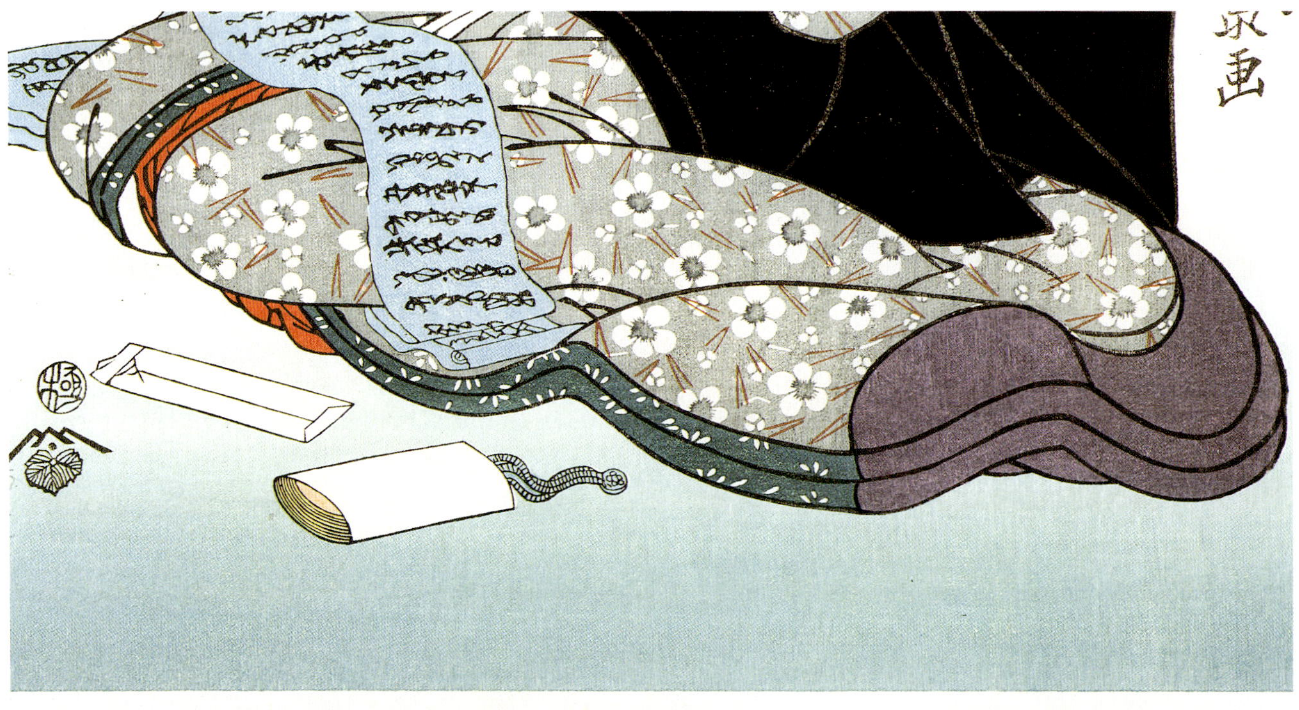

Detail of a modern reproduction of a print by Eisen. In the bottom margin is printed a label giving the names of the publisher, master blockcarver: Itoh Susumu, printer, and papermaker.

carve new blocks a fraction of a millimeter larger than the original compositions. This can be detected through careful measuring or by holding up to the light two prints (one an Edo-period print, one a modern reproduction) of the same composition.

These modern reproductions are meant to extend the enjoyment of woodblock color prints to a wider modern audience. The colors of Edo period prints, especially the many colors produced by fugitive organic pigments, have often faded or disappeared completely. The uneven rate at which pigments change color tends to further distort the overall impression given by an old print. At the same time, glossy photographic reproductions fail to convey the softness and harmony of tone achieved in printing on supple *washi*. Woodblock prints are meant to be looked at up close and (gently) handled. Few of us have opportunities actually to hold Edo-period prints that are preserved in museum storage or behind glass.

Of course, a modern reproduction of an Edo-period print loses something in the remaking. Some aspects of old *nishiki-e* cannot be duplicated. For example, printers can no longer acquire some of the inorganic pigments, banned because of their toxicity and consequent environmental hazards. Modern reproductions tend to require more woodblocks and impressions than the original print as modern craftsmen strive to copy certain effects or colors. This extra effort among other things results in a loss of vitality.

Moreover, the central problem remains unsolvable: what exactly to reproduce when making a copy of an extant Edo-period woodblock print. Modern craftsmen fall into two camps. Some strive to reproduce a print as it probably looked originally. Kajikawa Yoshio is one who believes in analyzing or working back from the present condition and the faded colors of a print to reproduce with traditional pigments the bright, vivid "feel" of the Edo period. Then, there are a few who think that rather than relying on guesswork, however well-informed, reproductions should more closely copy surviving originals. They reason that softer colors result in immediate effects closer to those prints the public has grown to like.

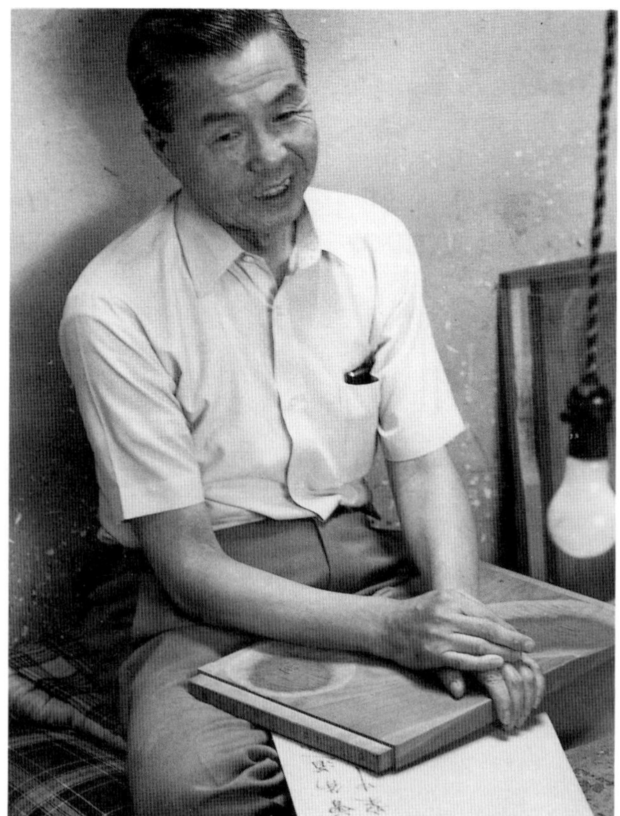

Printer Kajikawa Yoshio discusses traditional printmaking techniques and their future.

Modern reproductions using the traditional woodblock process of old *ukiyo-e* prints are expensive. Traditional materials like *hōsho* paper and the labor of various craftspeople do not come cheap. Because of their cost, reproductions of *nishiki-e* have not been popular with tourists and art-lovers from outside Japan. Those with interest and enough money wanted the real thing. Most rather settled for a book about *ukiyo-e* with offset reproductions. Modern Japanese taste and interior decor have never favored the display of *ukiyo-e*. Doctors, retired government workers and teachers in Japan, who bought *ukiyo-e* reproductions as collectibles in the 1960's and 1970's at department store exhibits or through home-sale schemes, have since turned to other things. In the early 1980's the bottom fell out of the *ukiyo-e* print reproduction market.

One hope of craftsmen who practice the full-color woodblock techniques is that a collaboration will develop between them and contemporary Japanese artists, especially those working with traditional Japanese themes and materials in the *nihon-ga* movement. Well known paintings by Higashiyama Kaii or Okamoto Dōgyū have been reinterpreted with the artist's cooperation in limited edition full-color woodblock prints. Leaving far behind the *ukiyo-e* style these prints use woodblock techniques to explore new effects of overprinting colors or the use of gold foil. Such prints, however, are only copies of paintings. For a collaboration to be really successful, contemporary artists need once again to design compositions expressly for the full-color woodblock medium.

Suggestions for Further Reading

This bibliography is by no means exhaustive, but lists books and articles I have found useful and which may prove helpful to the English-speaking reader.

First, comprehensive works that deal with Japanese woodblock prints and present extensive introductions to historical developments and technical aspects of traditional printmaking. (Any other titles by these scholars can be recommended).

Hillier, Jack *Japanese Colour Prints* (Phaidon Press, 1966)
        The Japanese Print: a New Approach (reissued by Charles E. Tuttle, 1960)
Hillier, Jack and Lawrence Smith
        Japanese Prints: 300 Years of Albums and Books (British Museum, 1980)
Illings, Richard *The Art of Japanese Prints* (John Calmann and Cooper, 1980)
Keyes, Roger *The Art of Surimono—In the Chester Beatty Library* (Sotheby, 1985)
        Surimono: Privately Published Prints in the Spencer Museum of Art (Kodansha, 1984)
Lane, Richard *Images from the Floating World* (G.P. Putnam's Sons, 1978)
Meech-Pekarik, Julia *The World of the Meiji Print* (Weatherhill, 1986)
The Theatrical Prints of the Torii Masters (Riccar and Honolulu Academy of Arts, 1977)

For an early (perhaps the earliest) account of the printmaking process in English, see "Tokuno's (1889) Description of Japanese Printmaking," edited by Peter Morse, in *Essays on Japanese Art Presented to Jack Hillier* (Robert G. Sawers, 1982). Finally, two works filled with illustrations about techniques: the encyclopedia—*Genshoku ukiyo-e daihyakka jiten* (especially vol. 11, 1982) and Sadamura Tadashi's photographic account of modern craftsmen re-printing from old woodblocks, *Ima Hokusai ga yomigaeru: Ukiyo-e hanga ga suriagaru made* (Kawade Shobōshinsha, 1987).

For information about pigments: Feller, Curran, and Bailie, "Identification of Traditional Organic Colorants Employed on Japanese Prints . . . ," in Roger Keyes, ed. *Japanese Woodblock Prints: The Ainsworth Collection* (Oberlin, 1984). Also look for articles by the research staff of the Freer Gallery, including John Winter and Elizabeth West Fitzhugh.

INDEX

abstract style: in prints, 20
actor prints, 11
ai, 37
aiban (format), 23
ai-gami, 37
alum, 38
anchoring block for printing, 41
Andō Enshi (carver), 25, 76
aniline dyes, 38
apprenticeship: 29, 35; today, 79
"*aratame*", 27
artist/designer, 14, 25, 32, 35
artisan, 14
artistic families/schools, 12
artist's master design/drawing, 25, 30
Asakusa temple: scene of, 76
associations (guilds) of artisans, 28, 35, 79

B

baren, 42–3, 45
beautiful women (prints of): 11, 16–7, 34; 19th c depictions, 19, 36; nude, 20; substituted in parodies, 8–9, 28–9
beni, 37
beni-e, 13
benigara, 37
benizuri-e, 13
berorinai, 38
Bigelow, William S.: 77
Bitchū, 23; map, 21
black (on prints), 12, 34
black-intensifier impression, 34, 60–1, 70–1
blind printing, 44
blockcarver's tools, 30–1; also: 9, 28
blockcarving techniques, 29–34
bokashi, 41
bookjackets (on illustrated popular fiction): 77; illus. 75
"brocade prints", 14
brushes: 38, 40–1; modern type, 45
Ippitsusai BUNCHŌ, 16
"Butterflies, Collection of", 17
buying public, of prints: 10–11, 75, 77–9; of reproductions, 81

C

calcium carbonate (see *gofun*), 37
carving techniques, 29–34
censorship, of publications/ prints: 10, 25–6, 27
censor's seal impressions, 27
chisels and mallets, 28, 30, 31
chōji, 37
chūban (format), 14, 23
collecting prints, 8, 80–1
colorants (see pigments), 37
coloring, Edo taste in: 38
colors, consistency in printing: 42–3, 44
commercial vs. privately commissioned prints, 14, 25
copying, of old prints: 80–1
copyright, 77
cracking, of woodblocks: 76–7

D

dai'ō, 38
dayflower pigment, 37
date symbols, on prints: 27, illus. 74–5
"decadence" (decline in 19th c print quality), 17–9
demand, for a print composition: 11, 44, 77–9
drawing (master design) for a print: 25

E

an edition: 44, 46; later editions, 32, 80
Edo, 10; map, 21
enju, 37
embossing, 44
empaku, 37
ezōshi, 79
egoyomi, 14–5
Eichizen, 21, 23
Keisai EISEN, 19, 79
Chōbunsai EISHI, 17, 44
Kikukawa EIZAN, 19
Emiya (publisher), 13
Endō Goryoku (blockcarver), 14
an engraver, 29

F

fabric, depiction of: 11, 17, 44
fading, of print colors: 37–8, 80–1
"Famous Sights of the Eastern Capital", 76
finishing block, 34, 68–9
forgeries, 24, 80–1
formats (typical for prints): 23–4
"Fuji", "Views of Mt." : 18
full-color printing, history: 14–20

G

GAKUTEI, 17
gamboge, 37
gampi (paper), 24
gasenshi (paper), 24
gauffrage, 44
geisha (subject matter), 19, 27
Gifts of the Ebb Tide, 24
glue, 37
gofun, 37
gold and silver, printing: 44
gougers, 30, 36
guide marks (*kentō*), 13, 30, 34–5
guilds (organisations) of artisans: 29, 35, 79

H

hairstyles, printing of: 11, 34
hanmoto, 25
Hakusei (patron), 14
Suzuki HARUNOBU, 14–5
Hashiguchi Goyō, 20
hikitsuke, 13, 30
Andō HIROSHIGE, 18, 38
Hishiya Kimbei (publisher), 77
Totoya HOKKEI, 17; see also Uoya (publisher)
Katsushika HOKUSAI: 18, 19, 38; book illus. by: 25, 27, 76, 77
hōsho (paper), 23, 44

hosoban (format), 23
hosokawa (paper), 24
humidity, effects on printing: 36, 38; on pigments: 37–8

I

Ichikawa Danjurō, print of, 11
indigo 37
inks, see pigments, 37–8
ippai, 44
Itoh Shinsui, 20
Itoh Susumu: biog. 79; 31, 33, 80
Iyo-bōsho and *masa* (paper), 23
Izumi Ichibei (publisher), 27

J

Japan, map of: 21

K

"Kabuki Actor", print of: 11
Kajikawa Yoshio: biog. 79; 41, 45, 81
Kamigata, 12, 75; see map, 21
karazuri, 44
Katsushika, see HOKUSAI
Kawachiya Mohei (publisher), 76
kentō: 13; carving, 30; marks removed, 72; re-cutting, 34–5
the keyblock: 30–1, 32, 33; also illus. 34, 25, 27
keyblock proof, 47
kihada, 37
kimedashi, 44
"*kiwame*", 27
Kobayashi KIYOCHIKA, 19
Torii KIYONAGA, 16
Torii KIYONOBU, 12
knives, 30, 31
-*kō* (in signatures), 14
kōzo, 21–2, 23, 24
Isoda KORYŪSAI, 16
Toyoharu KUNICHIKA, 19
Utagawa KUNIMASA, 11
Utagawa KUNISADA (or TOYOKUNI III.): 18–9; prints of: title page, 8–9, 36, 74–5, 78–9
Utagawa KUNIYOSHI, 18
kusashio, 37
kyōka (poetry): 14, 17; also illus. 76

L

"lacquer prints", 13
landscape, 12, 18, 19
lead, 37
"A Look Along Both Banks of the River Sumida", 25

M

Maekawa Zenbei (publisher), 25
margins (of prints): info. in, 14, 27, 80; trimming, 6–7, 72
"Making Edo's Famous Souvenir the Full-color Print: Shown as a Parody of Rice Cultivation": 28, 39, 43, 72–3
market, for prints: see buying public/ demand

masa (paper), 22–3
Okumura MASANOBU, 13
Meiji period prints, 19, 38; ex. of, 6
metalic-powder pigments, 38
mica, 17, 38, 44
middlemen sellers, 26–7, 74–5; also illus. 16
mino (paper), 24
mitate, 19
mitsumata, 24
modern prints, 19–20, 81–2
moisture content: of blocks, 36, 41, 44; of paper, 38
"Morning of the New Year in Color", 16
Hishikawa MORONOBU, 10, 12
mounting prints: 72–3; paper for, 24
moveable type, 12
multiples, of prints: 24

N

nagaban (surimono format), 23
New Year's season: picture calendars 14; sale of prints: 16, 74
nikawa, 36; also, 13, 38
nishiki-e, def. 14, 75
Nishimuraya Yohachi (publisher), 16, 72
nishinouchi (paper)

O

ōban (format), 16, 23–4
ōbōsho (sheet size), 23–4
ōhirobōsho (sheet size), 23
Onchi Kōshiro, 20
"One of the Souvenirs of Edo: Shop for *ezōshi*", 79
Otaki (Fukui), 21
overprinting colors, 34

P

painted colors (on prints), 13–4
painting, in *ukiyo-e*, 10
paints (traditional), 37
paper: format/size chart, 23; moisture content, 38; new, in bundles, 6–7; types, 22–24
papermaking, 21–2, 24
paper mulberry, 21
"A Parody of Samurai, Farmers, Artisans, and Merchants in the Latest Fashions: Artisans/Merchants", illus.: title page, 9, 36, 74–5
"The Passionate Type", 17
paste, 30, 41
patronage, 10, 14
perspective, techniques of: 12, 18
picture calendars, 14–5
pigments, 37–8, 80
"Pleasures of the East(ern Capital)", 26–7
plugs (plugging) in woodblocks: 29, 32–3, 76
poetry (*kyōka*) groups, 14, 17
"The Preservation of Ukiyo-e Woodblock-print Carving and Printing", Ass. of: 79
"Primitives", see early printmaking, 12–3
printing techniques, 42–4
printer's work-area: illus. 36; 41, 45
printing press, 12, 42

"Producing Full-color Woodblock Prints", 6–7
the proofs (of prints), 32–3, 35
Prussian blue, 38
public, for prints: 10, 75, 77, 79
publisher's mark (on prints), 27
publishing prints 25–7, 77; also, 12, 18, 79

R

realism, in *ukiyo-e*: 12, 16
registration, of colors in printing: 13, 35–6, 42; see *kentō*
re-inking of woodblock, 42
reproductions (of prints), 80–1
retail shops, for prints 75, 78–9
re-touching, 80
"rice paper", 21
rice-starch paste, 21, 30, 41

S

saturation of woodblock, 44
Saga-bon, 12
screen (papermaking), 22, 24
selling prints: 16, 72–5, 77–9; today, 80–1
shading, 12, 41
Tōshūsai SHARAKU, 16–7
shark skin, 40
sheet sizes (paper), 23
shikishi (surimono format), 17, 23
Shimano Tokusaburō and Shintarō, 78–9
shio, 37
shōbōsho (sheet size), 23
shu, 37
Katsukawa SHUN'EI, 10, 17
Kubota SHUNMAN, 17
Katsukawa SHUNSHŌ, 16
shop logo, 27
the signature: of artist, 25; of carver/printer, 14, 75, 80
single-sheet prints, 12
sizes (formats) of prints, 23
sizing: 38–9, 80; also, illus. 6, 9
"Snow", 19, 32, 46–71
starch: papermaking, 21; paste, 30, 41
style, of *ukiyo-e*: 10, 12, 41
storage, of blocks: 77
Suharaya Mohei and Ihachi (publishers), 76
sumi: 37, 42–3; also, 12, 32
"Sumidagawa", "A Look Along . . .": 25
"Sumo Wrestlers", 10
surimono: 14, 17; also, 23, 38, 44
Suzuki Nanrei, 19

T

tan, 12, 37
"Tōkaidō," "Fifty-three Stations on": 18
tools (illustrated): for carving, 30–1; printing, 36, 40, 42
Torii school, 12, 79
torinoko (paper), 24
tororo-aoi starch, 21
Hosoki TOSHIICHI, 6–7
Utagawa TOYOHARU, 18
TOYOKUNI III., see KUNISADA: 8
Ishikawa TOYONOBU, 13

trial impressions (proofs): 32–3, 35, 42
trimming prints, 6–7, 27, 72
tsuke, 29
Tsuruya Kiemon (publisher): 29, 72–3
Tsutaya Jūzaburō I. and II. (publisher): 16–7, 26–7, 76–77
tsuyugusa, 37–8
tumeric root, 37

U

Uemura Kichiemon, 13
uki-e, 19
ukon, 37
Uoya Eikichi (publisher): 8, 74–5
Utagawa school, 18; also see, KUNISADA
ukiyo-e, definition of: 10–11; style, 12, 41
Kitagawa UTAMARO, 16–7; prints of, 17, 28, 39, 43, 72–3

W

washi, 21–4
watermarks (print paper): 22, 24
wheat paste, 30
white, printing of: 37
the woodblock: 29, 34–5; damage/warping, 76–7; plugging, 32–3, 76; reinforcement, 31, 77; storage, 6–7, 77; wearing-down, 44
woodblock carving techniques, 30–4

Y

yamato-e, 12
Yokokawa Chōchiku (carver), 75
Utagawa YOSHIIKU, 78–9
Tsukioka YOSHITOSHI, 19
"Young Girl in a Summer Shower", 14–5
Yumoto Kōshi (printer), 14

Z

zumi, 37